How to Create Language Experts With
Literary Terms

Codi Hrouda and Emma McInerney
with Lyle Lee Jenkins

I0568196

My Book of Favorite Sight Words

By: _____

School: _____

Teacher: _____

Date: _____

My Book of Inferential Questions

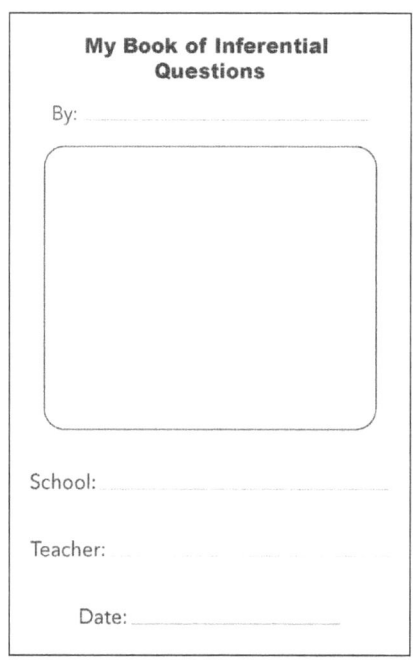

By: _____

School: _____

Teacher: _____

Date: _____

My Book of Homophones

By: _____

School: _____

Teacher: _____

Date: _____

My Book of Alliterations

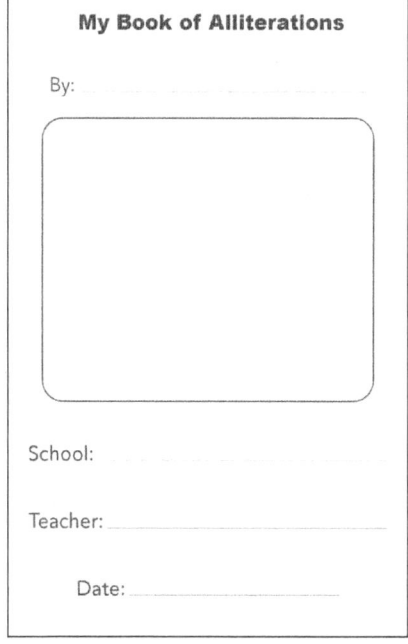

By: _____

School: _____

Teacher: _____

Date: _____

My Book of Two Syllable Words

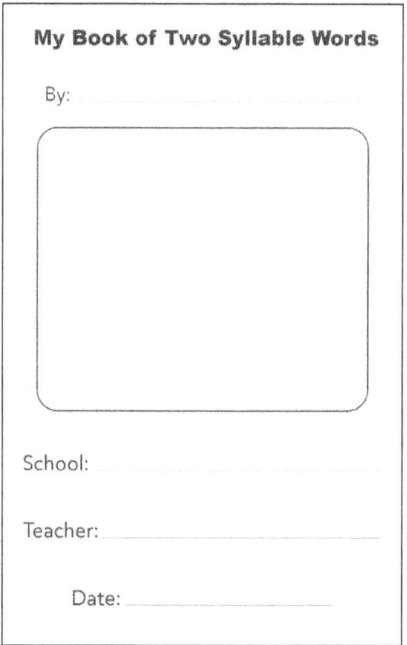

By: _____

School: _____

Teacher: _____

Date: _____

Perfect School Collection™

Copyright © 2023 by Codi Hrouda, Emma McInerney and Lyle Lee Jenkins

All rights reserved. No part of this publication may be reproduced, distributed, or transmitted in any form or by any means, including photocopying, recording, or other electronic or mechanical methods, without the prior written permission of the publisher, LtoJ Press, except in the case of brief quotations embodied in critical reviews and certain other non-commercial uses permitted by copyright law.

To contact the authors regarding keynotes, workshops or bulk orders, visit LtoJ.net/Contact

ISBN: 978-1-956457-64-3

Book Design & Graphics: Christy Courtright, Christy's Customs LLC
Quality Assurance Manager: Kelly Lippert
Publishing Consultant: Martha Bullen, Bullen Publishing Services
Distribution Coordinator: Maggie McLaughlin

Printed in the United States of America

The Perfect School Collection™

How to Create a Perfect School by Lyle Lee Jenkins

How to Create a Perfect Home School by Lyle Lee Jenkins and Kelly Hawkinson Lippert

Perfect School Collection™ Resources

How to Create Math Experts series by Peggy McLean and Lyle Lee Jenkins

How to Create Math Experts with Fluency Quizzes by Peggy McLean and Lyle Lee Jenkins

How to Create Math Experts with Math Standards Quizzes by Peggy McLean, Laura Hayes and Lyle Lee Jenkins

How to Create a Math Foundation for Future Math Experts by Lyle Lee Jenkins

How to Create Bible Experts: Genesis to Revelation by Richard Douglas Junior Jenkins with Lyle Lee Jenkins

Early Readers

Bible Patterns for Young Readers series by Lyle Lee Jenkins

Aesop Patterns for Young Readers series by Lyle Lee Jenkins

Young Authors

Wordless Books for Young Authors series by Jim Chansler and Lyle Lee Jenkins

Special Project

All About Henry: Rich Widower of Savannah Valley by Lyle Lee Jenkins

CONTENTS

Purchasers of *How to Create Language Experts with Literary Terms* may utilize the QR code provided at the end of the book to download student booklets from this book at no extra cost. Both the print and downloaded copies are protected by copyright laws.

INTRODUCTION

The philosophy behind these booklets is that they are student-led, and elementary (K - 6) standards driven. In other words, students can independently complete much of the materials they are expected to learn in school with occasional pre-teaching.

The booklets are designed with a left-brain/right-brain balance. The back cover is a right-brain activity and the inside pages are clearly left-brain. The page prior to each grade level gives parents and teachers background knowledge and suggestions to successfully support their students and children through the booklets.

In order to create and assemble the booklets, parents and teachers can scan the QR code provided at the end of the book to download digital copies. To ensure proper printing, please utilize double sided printing and set your printer to "flip" on the short edge. The front page will be the front and back cover of the booklet. We have also included some bonus booklets within this series to support additional literary term exploration.

Enjoy,

Codi Hrouda, Emma McInerney and Lyle Lee Jenkins

KINDERGARTEN BOOKLET DIRECTIONS

Depending on your student or child's' reading ability, directions may need to be read to them.

My Book of Titles and Authors:
Students will need access to a multitude of texts and coloring supplies. They may need modeling of where to find the title and author on a book cover for this booklet.

My Book of Comprehension:
Students will need to have access to their favorite picture book and coloring supplies. They are given the option to write or tell an adult what is happening in the pictures within the chosen book.

My Book of Sentences with Question Marks:
Students will need to have access to their favorite books. They may need to be pre-taught punctuation and given an example of when to use the punctuation.

My Book of Sentences with Exclamation Marks:
Students will need to have access to their favorite books. They may need to be pre-taught punctuation and given an example of when to use the punctuation.

My Book of Uppercase Letters:
Students may need modeling of how to write uppercase letters on primary dotted lines.

My Book of Lowercase Letters:
Students may need modeling of how to write lowercase letters on primary dotted lines.

My Book of Rhyming Words:
Students may need to be pre-taught what rhyming means and given examples of rhyming words.

My Book of Two Syllable Words:
Students may need to be pre-taught what two syllable words are and given examples/ strategies on how to identify syllables within a word.
Example: clapping out each syllable

Student booklets are available via the QR code at the end of the book

Draw your own book cover with a title and author.

My Book of Titles and Authors

By: ______________________

School: ______________________

Teacher: ______________________

Date: ______________________

Write the titles and authors of your favorite books

Titles	Authors
______	______
______	______
______	______
______	______
______	______

Draw your favorite book cover with the title and author.

Student booklets are available via the QR code at the end of the book

Draw pictures to tell a story of your favorite memory

My Book of Comprehension

By: _____

School: _____

Teacher: _____

Date: _____

Find four pictures in your favorite picture book and tell a grown-up or write what is happening in each picture.

Picture 1:

Picture 2:

Picture 3:

Picture 4:

Write sentences with question marks:

_____

_____

_____

_____

My Book of Sentences with Question Marks

By: _____

School: _____

Teacher: _____

Date: _____

Circle the question marks in each sentence below:

1. What is your cat's name?

2. I like dogs.

3. Who is taller?

4. When is your birthday?

5. We got ice cream!

6. How old are you?

7. I am two years old.

Copy sentences with question marks from your favorite book:

_____

_____

_____

_____

Student booklets are available via the QR code at the end of the book

Write sentences with exclamation marks:

_____

_____

_____

_____

My Book of Sentences with Exclamation Marks

By: _____

School: _____

Teacher: _____

Date: _____

Circle the exclamation marks in each sentence below:

1. What is your name?

2. We got ice cream!

3. I did it!

4. I do not like cats.

5. Look at me!

6. I am sad.

7. I can ride my bike!

Copy sentences with exclamation marks from your favorite book:

_____

_____

_____

_____

Draw a picture of something that starts with the uppercase letter. Then write the word using the uppercase letter.

G

My Book of Uppercase Letters

By: _____

D

School: _____

Teacher: _____

Date: _____

Circle the uppercase letters below:

Write the word in uppercase letters:

A b C D e f

cot _____

g H I j k l M

pin _____

N o P q R s t

birthday _____

U v W x y Z

soccer _____

Student booklets are available via the QR code at the end of the book

Draw a picture of something that starts with the lowercase letter. Then write the word using lowercase letter.

f

b

My Book of Lowercase Letters

By: _____

School: _____

Teacher: _____

Date: _____

Circle the lowercase letters below:

Write the word in lowercase letters:

B p x Y r u

Q s l M c l N

e A f I H k t

R o z G E a

DOG
_____
- - - - - - - - - - - - - - - -

BED
_____
- - - - - - - - - - - - - - - -

CATFISH
_____
- - - - - - - - - - - - - - - -

KINDERGARTEN
_____
- - - - - - - - - - - - - - - -

Write a list of words you know, then write a word that rhymes with each of them.

Words	Rhyming Words
_____	_____
_____	_____
_____	_____
_____	_____
_____	_____

My Book of Rhyming Words

By: _____

School: _____

Teacher: _____

Date: _____

Draw a line to match the rhyming words.

Cat   Cry

Dig   Cup

Mop   Mat

Dog   Raincoat

Up   Fog

Sailboat Big

Butterfly Hop

Fill in the missing letters to make a word that rhymes with each underlined word.

<u>Set</u>

G e _

g   t   w

<u>Bad</u>

S a _

d   s   k

List the names of your favorite songs and circle those that are multi-syllable words.

_____

_____

_____

_____

_____

My Book of Two Syllable Words

By: _____

School: _____

Teacher: _____

Date: _____

Read each word and write the number of syllables it has:

pen _____   rocket _____

helmet _____   capital _____

let _____   picnic _____

name _____   hop _____

basketball _____   napkin _____

Read a book and write any two-syllable words you find

_____

_____

_____

_____

_____

GRADE 1
BOOKLET DIRECTIONS

Depending on your student or child's' reading ability, directions may need to be read to them.

My Book of Favorite Sight Words:
Students may need to be pre-taught what sight words are and given examples of sight words.

My Book of Words in the Same Family:
Within the booklet, the term "word family" is used. This means words that can be categorized together.

My Book of Main Character and Setting:
Students will need to have access to their favorite picture books and coloring supplies.

My Book of Important Events in the Story:
Students will need to have access to their favorite picture books and coloring supplies.

My Book of Connections:
Students will need to have access to their favorite fiction and nonfiction book.

My Book of Characters That are the Same and Different:
Students will need to have access to two fiction books.

My Book of _____ Facts:
Students are to chose the topic they would like to investigate and fill the topic into the title. Access to non-fiction books will be needed for this booklet.

My Book of Predictions:
Students will need to have access to a nonfiction book and coloring supplies.

Write a story using as many sight words as you can

My Book of Favorite Sight Words

By: _____

School: _____

Teacher: _____

Date: _____

Sight words - Words that cannot be sounded out so you need to know them by sight.

Read and sound out all the words below. Circle the sight words:

From   All   Them

Toss   Been   Did

Who   Does   Skip

The   Coat   Shout

Read a book and find as many sight words as you can. List them below without writing them more than once.

_____ _____

_____ _____

_____ _____

_____ _____

_____ _____

_____ _____

_____ _____

Student booklets are available via the QR code at the end of the book

List two holidays you celebrate and write their word families. Circle any words that could fit under either holiday.

Holiday 1:   Holiday 2:

_____   _____

_____   _____

_____   _____

_____   _____

_____   _____

My Book of Words in the Same Family

By: _____

School: _____

Teacher: _____

Date: _____

List words that have something in common with your word on the front creating a word family. (Ex. Books - pages, shelf, cover)

_____   _____

_____   _____

_____   _____

_____   _____

_____   _____

_____   _____

Use the bold word to create a word family

Outerspace

_____   _____

_____   _____

Animals

_____   _____

_____   _____

Food

_____   _____

_____   _____

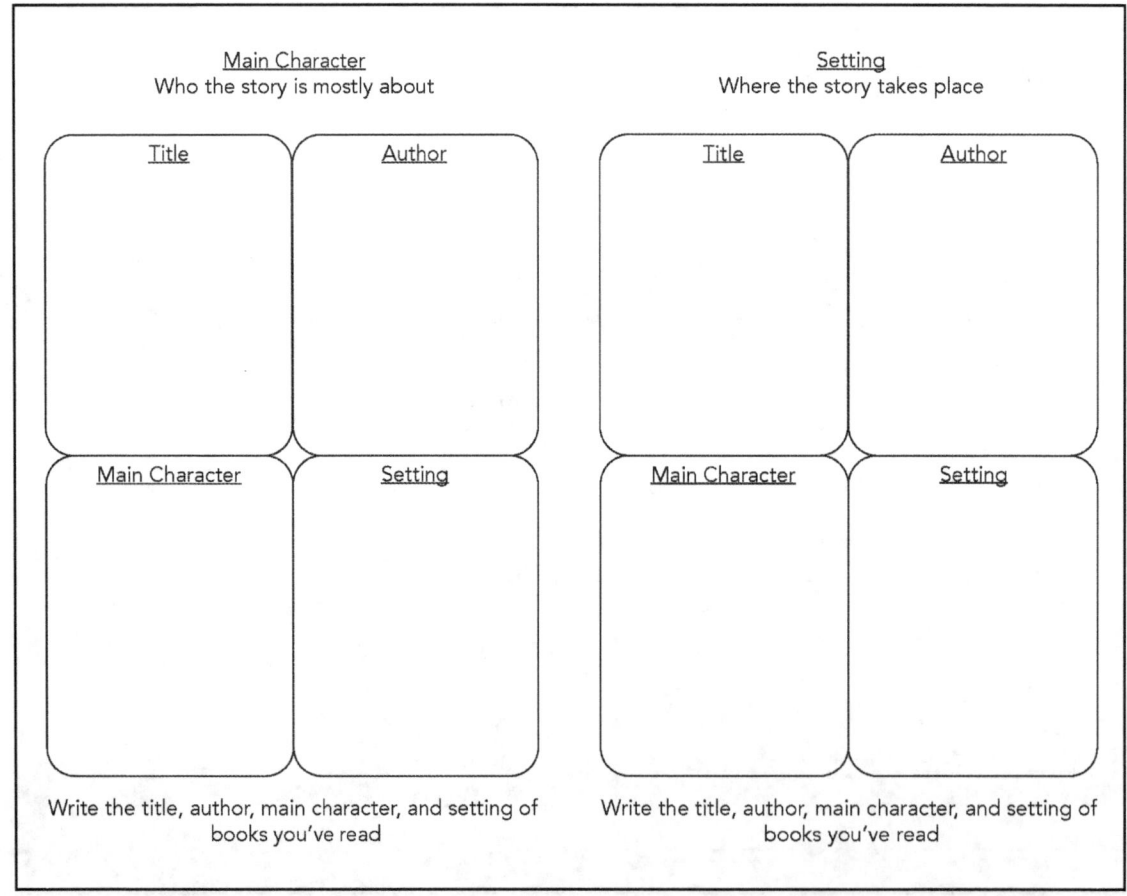

Draw your own main character and setting

My Book of Main Characters and Settings

By: _____

School: _____

Teacher: _____

Date: _____

Main Character
Who the story is mostly about

Setting
Where the story takes place

Title

Author

Title

Author

Main Character

Setting

Main Character

Setting

Write the title, author, main character, and setting of books you've read

Write the title, author, main character, and setting of books you've read

Student booklets are available via the QR code at the end of the book

Write and draw about an important event in your life

My Book of Important Events

By: _____

School: _____

Teacher: _____

Date: _____

Read two books.
Then draw and write three important events

Book 1 Title: _____

Book 2 Title: _____

Tell how you connect to the main character from a fiction book:

My Book of Connections

By: _____

School: _____

Teacher: _____

Date: _____

Read two books and list the important facts or events you read about.
Then complete the sentence starters

Non-Fiction Book Title

Fiction Book Title

My connection is...

This story reminds me of...

Student booklets are available via the QR code at the end of the book

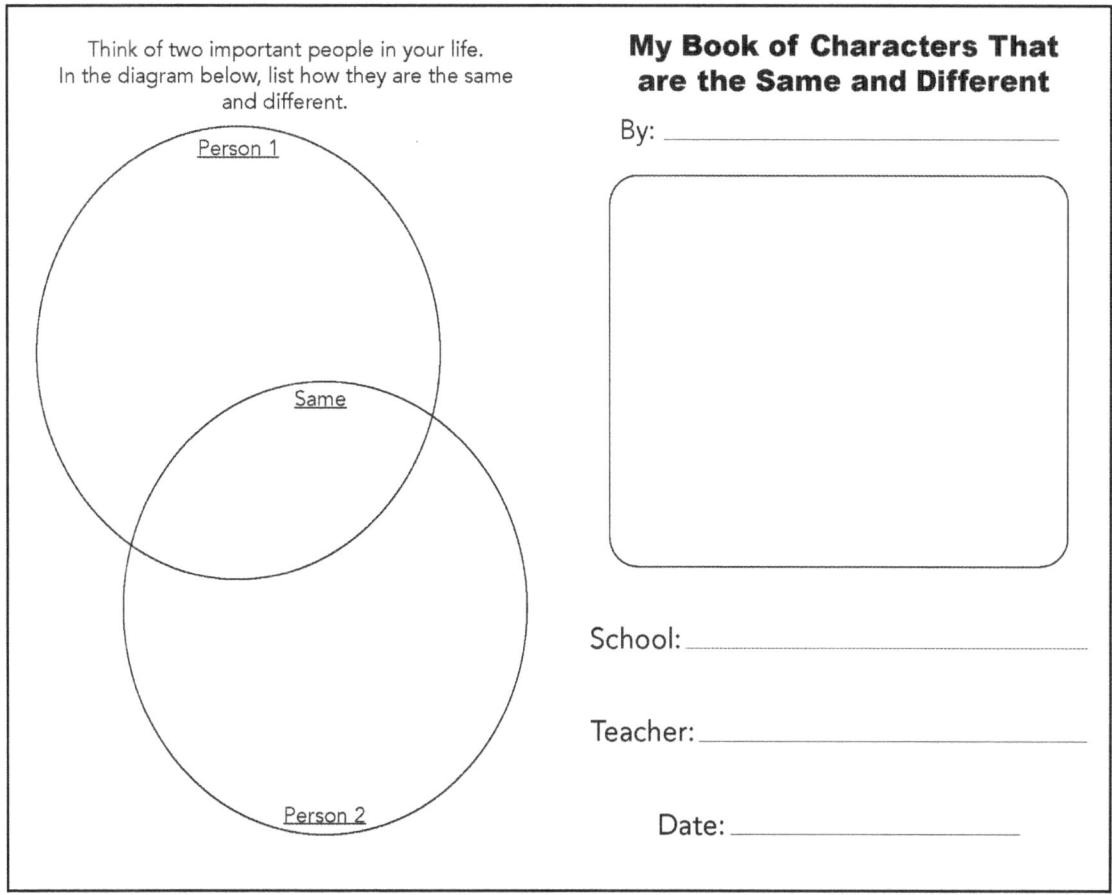

Think of two important people in your life. In the diagram below, list how they are the same and different.

Person 1

Same

Person 2

My Book of Characters That are the Same and Different

By: _____

School: _____

Teacher: _____

Date: _____

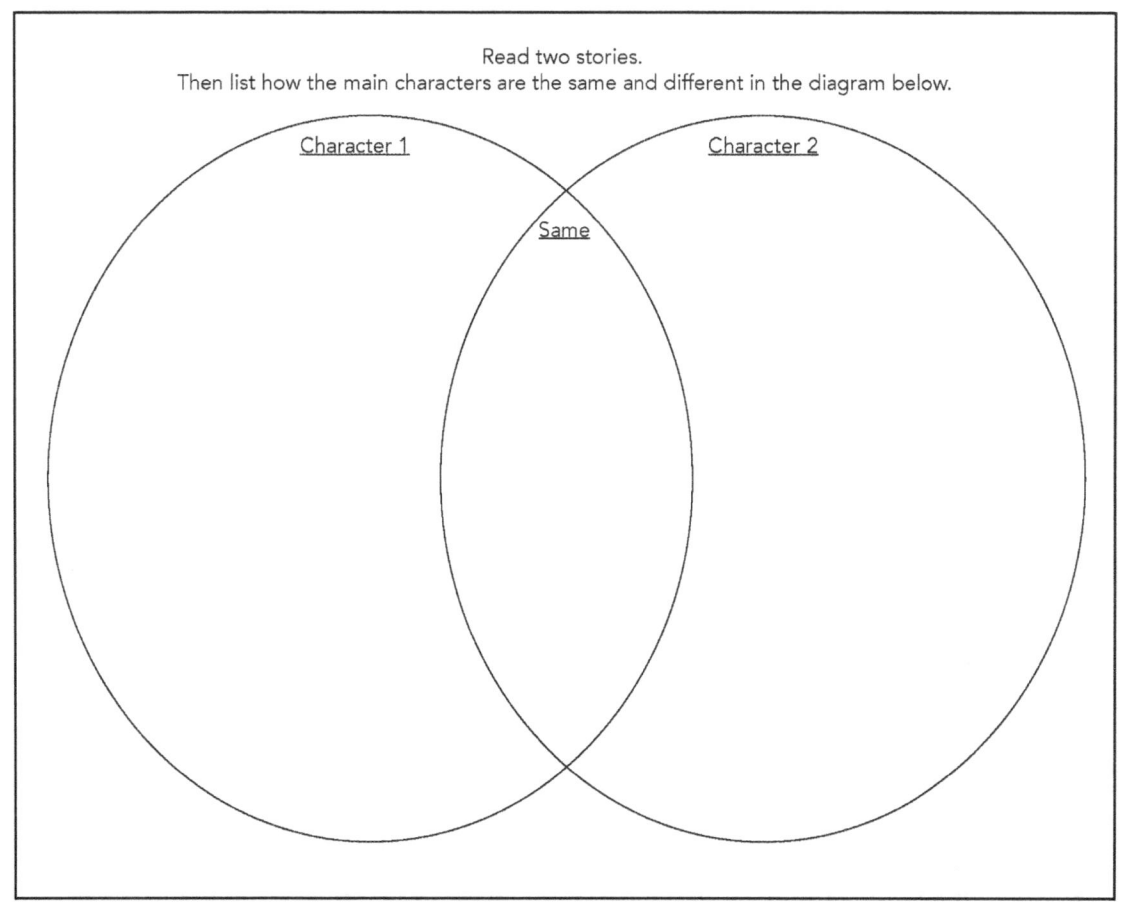

Read two stories.
Then list how the main characters are the same and different in the diagram below.

Character 1

Character 2

Same

Student booklets are available via the QR code at the end of the book

List facts about yourself:

My Book of ____________ Facts
(topic)

By: ____________

School: ____________

Teacher: ____________

Date: ____________

Read two books and list the important facts or events you read about.

Non-Fiction Book Title

Fiction Book Title

Student booklets are available via the QR code at the end of the book

Pretend you are writing a book about your favorite memory. Create a title, picture(s), and heading to help the reader predict what your book is about.

My Book of Predictions

By: _____

Title: _____

Picture(s):

School: _____

Teacher: _____

Heading: _____

Date: _____

Using a non-fiction book, find the following text features and make a prediction of what the book will be about.

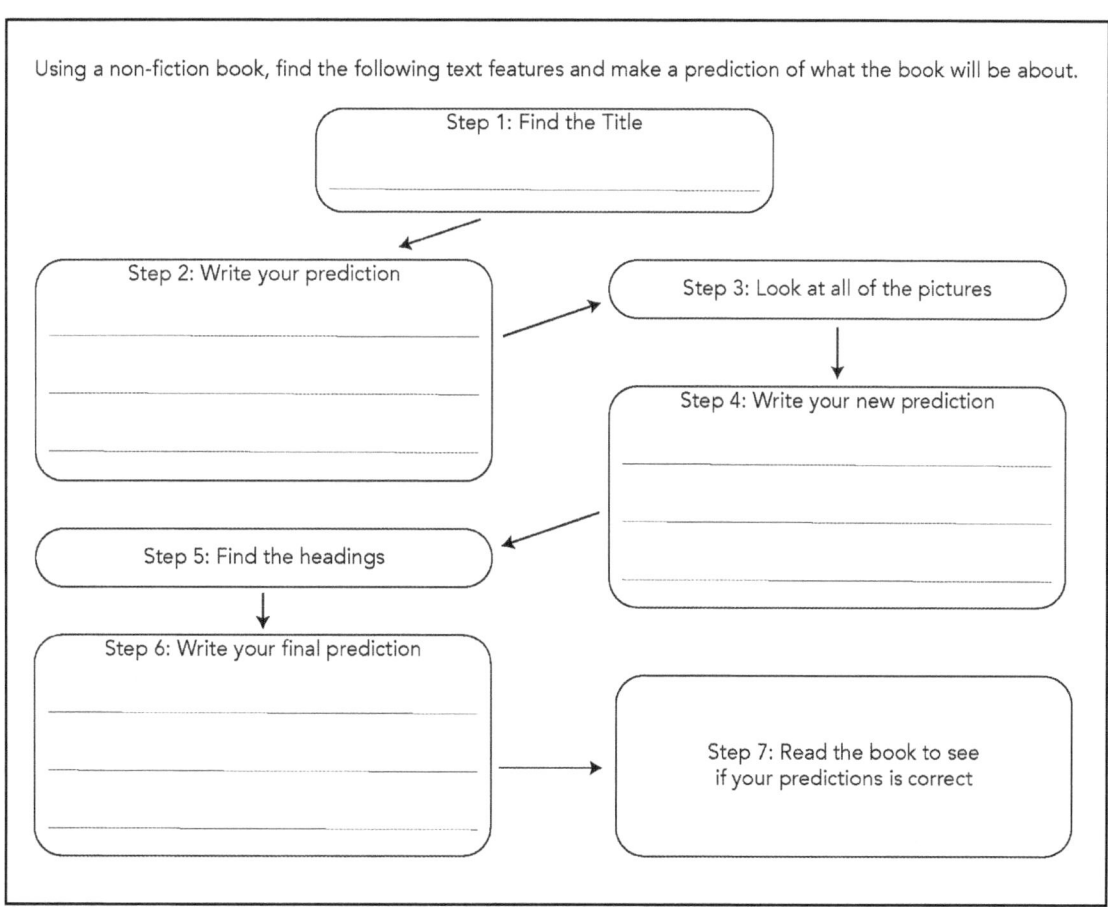

Step 1: Find the Title
_____

Step 2: Write your prediction
_____
_____
_____

Step 3: Look at all of the pictures

Step 4: Write your new prediction
_____
_____
_____

Step 5: Find the headings

Step 6: Write your final prediction
_____
_____
_____

Step 7: Read the book to see if your predictions is correct

GRADE 2
BOOKLET DIRECTIONS

My Book of Compound Words:
Students may need to be pre-taught what compound words are and given examples. Access to books that contain compound words will be needed for this booklet.

My Book of Prefixes and Suffixes:
Students may need to be pre-taught what prefixes and suffixes are and given examples. Access to books that contain prefixes and suffixes may be needed for this booklet.

My Book of Synonyms:
Students may need to be pre-taught what synonyms are and given examples. Access to their favorite books and song titles will be needed for this booklet.

My Book of Antonyms:
Students may need to be pre-taught what antonyms are and given examples. Access to their favorite books and song titles will be needed for this booklet.

My Book of Problems and Solutions:
Students will need to have access to fiction books.

My Book of the "W" Questions:
Students may need to be pre-taught the "W" questions (who, what, when, where and why), and why they are important for comprehension. Access to fiction books will be needed for this booklet.

My Book of Cultures That are the Same and Different:
Access to fiction books with similar plots with different cultural perspectives will be needed for this booklet. Students may need help interviewing a friend about their favorite holiday.

Some books we suggest:
*Cinderella By Disney Book Group and **The Rough-Face Girl** by Rafe Martin*
*Goldilocks and the Three Bears By: James Marshall and **Goldy Luck and the Three Pandas** by Natasha Yim*

My Book of Author's Purpose:
Students may need to be pre-taught on the ways authors write (persuade, inform, entertain). Access to books that are written for three different authors' purposes will be needed fr this booklet.

My Book of Lessons Learned:
Students will need to have access to fiction books.

List as many compound words as you can think of:

My Book of Compound Words

By: _____

School: _____

Teacher: _____

Date: _____

Fill in the blank to create a compound word:

_____ball

_____light

cross_____

_____body

water_____

fire_____

While reading a book, list any compound words you find:

Student booklets are available via the QR code at the end of the book

Find or create words that have BOTH
a prefix and a suffix:

....

....

....

_____   _____

_____   _____

_____   _____

_____   _____

My Book of Prefixes and Suffixes

By: ....

School: _____

Teacher: _____

Date: _____

Use the definitions to fill in the correct prefix
for each word:

<u>re</u> - again
<u>pre</u> - before
<u>un</u> - not

_____school   _____fair

_____turn   _____pare

_____able   _____common

Circle the words where two or more prefixes
can be used:

cook   dress   warm

do   lock   aware

Rewrite each word using the correct suffix.
*Remember some base words may need to be changed

<u>-s / -es</u> - more than one

fox   book

_____   _____

worry   way

_____   _____

Fill in the blank with the correct word using -ed or -ing
<u>-ed</u> - happen<u>ed</u> in the past
<u>-ing</u> - happen<u>ing</u> now

The rabbit _____ in the yard.
                    (hop)

My mom is _____ about the storm.
                  (worry)

The man _____ to the police.
                (lie)

Create a list of your favorite book titles.
Recreate parts of the title using synonyms

Book Title	New Title

_____ | _____

_____ | _____

_____ | _____

_____ | _____

_____ | _____

_____ | _____

My Book of Synonyms

By: _____

School: _____

Teacher: _____

Date: _____

Match words that are synonyms

Synonyms - words that have the same meaning

laugh   hurt

harm   mistakes

center   giggle

error   middle

love   adore

Rewrite the sentences using the synonym of the underlined word.

My grandma is <u>wealthy</u>.

_____

Susan is a good <u>pal</u>.

_____

I was very <u>tardy</u> to school.

_____

The bad <u>odor</u> is coming from the sacks.

_____

Student booklets are available via the QR code at the end of the book

Create a list of your favorite song titles.
Recreate parts of the title using antonyms.

Song Title	New Title
_____	_____
_____	_____
_____	_____
_____	_____
_____	_____
_____	_____

My Book of Antonyms

By: _____

School: _____

Teacher: _____

Date: _____

Match words that are antonyms.

Antonyms - words that have the opposite meaning

cold   odd

true   subtract

happy   hot

add   sad

even   false

Rewrite the sentences using the antonym of the underlined word.

Today, it is cold outside.

_____

The teacher asked the boy to add the numbers.

_____

The boat was sinking.

_____

She smiled at him.

_____

Read a book and identify the problem and solution.
Create a new solution to the problem.

**My Book of Problems
and Solutions**

Problem:

_____

_____

By: _____

Solution:

_____

_____

New Solution:

_____

_____

School:_____

Teacher:_____

Date:_____

Read two books. While reading, write down the character's main problem.
After reading, describe how the character solved the problem.

Title of Book One	Title of Book Two

Problem:

_____

_____

_____

Solution:

_____

_____

_____

Problem:

_____

_____

_____

Solution:

_____

_____

_____

Student booklets are available via the QR code at the end of the book

Read a book. Then create and answer "W" questions about the book.

My Book of the "W" Questions

By: _____

School: _____

Teacher: _____

Date: _____

Read two books.
Answer the "W" questions below.

Book 1

Who is the main character?

_____

What is the problem in the story?

_____

Where is the story taking place?

_____

Why did the character have this problem?

_____

Book 2

Who is the main character?

_____

What is the problem in the story?

_____

Where is the story taking place?

_____

Why did the character have this problem?

_____

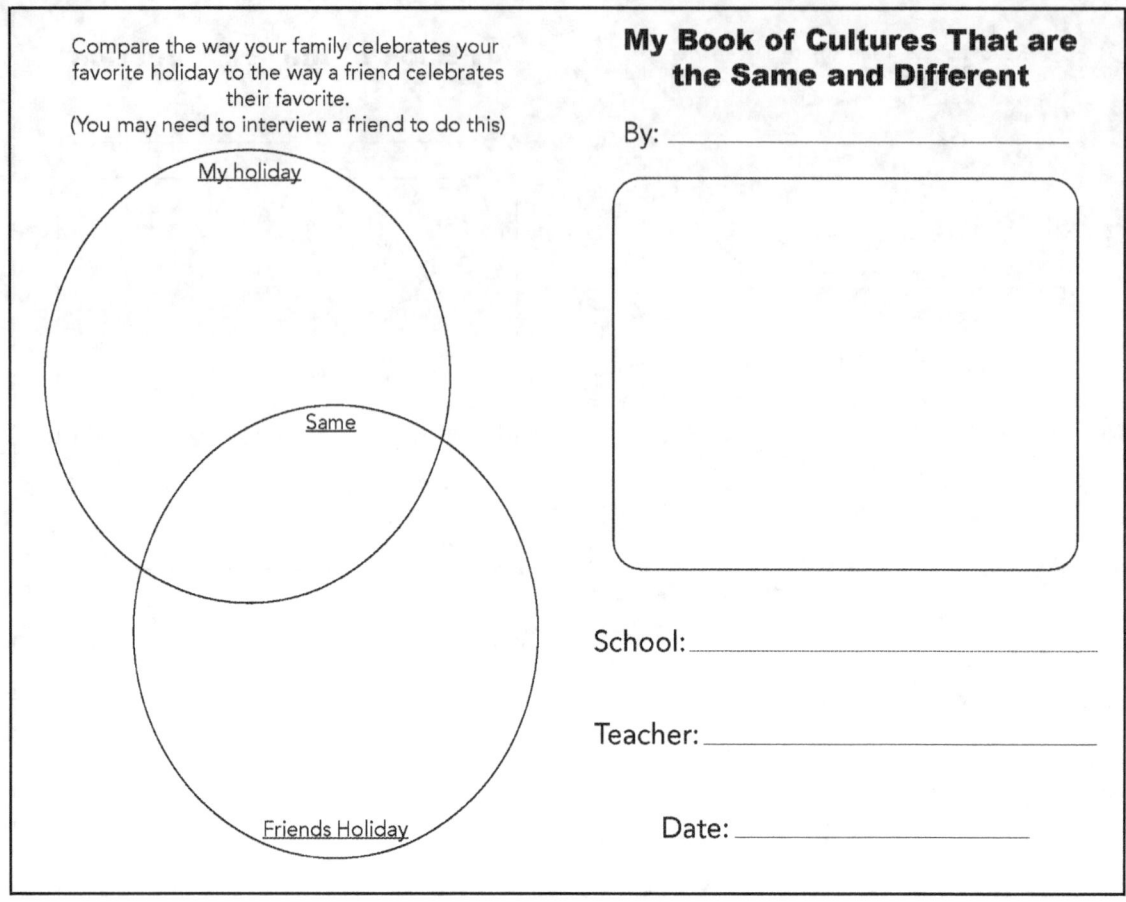

Compare the way your family celebrates your favorite holiday to the way a friend celebrates their favorite.
(You may need to interview a friend to do this)

My holiday

Same

Friends Holiday

My Book of Cultures That are the Same and Different

By: _____

School: _____

Teacher: _____

Date: _____

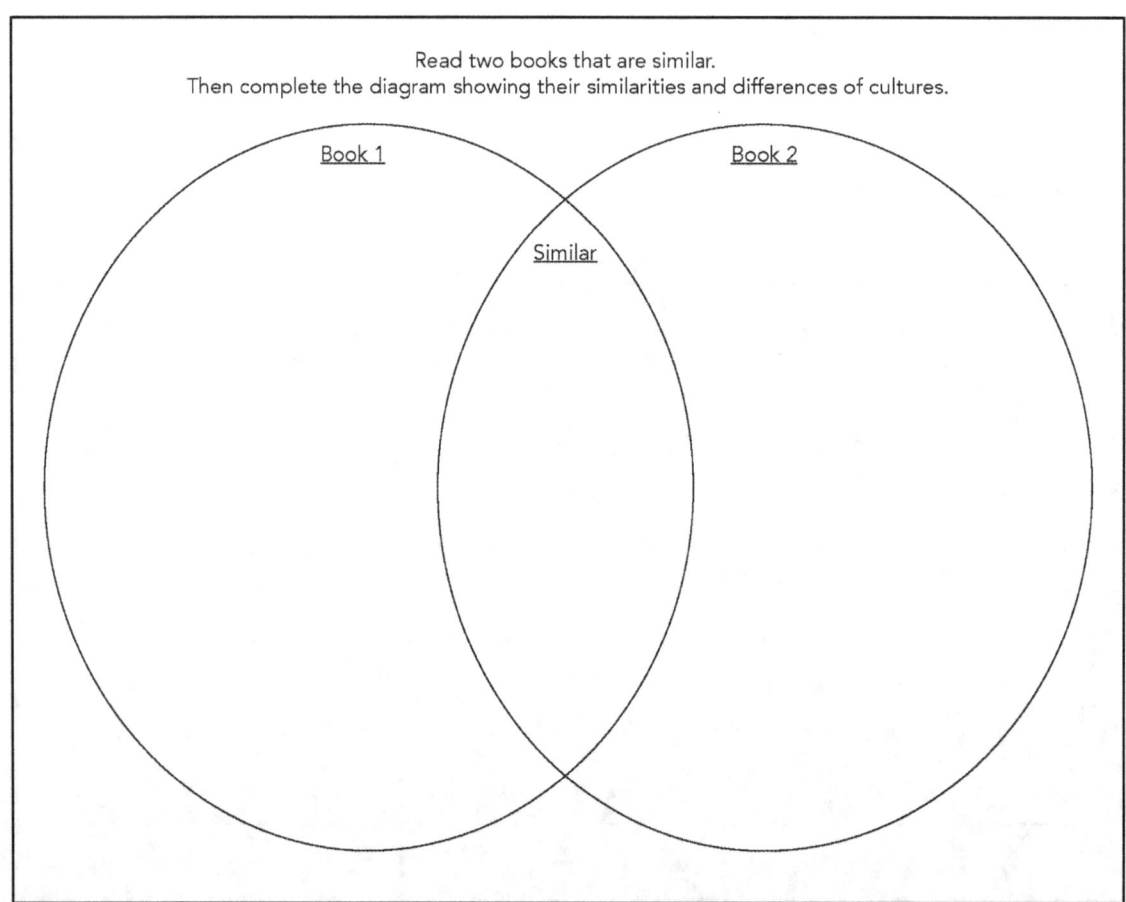

Read two books that are similar.
Then complete the diagram showing their similarities and differences of cultures.

Book 1

Similar

Book 2

List titles of texts that have more than one author's purpose.

My Book of Author's Purposes

By: _____

School: _____

Teacher: _____

Date: _____

Authors write for different purposes. Below are three purposes that authors use. Choose words from the word bank below that match each purpose

| Dictionary | Fairytales | Advertisements |

| Comics | Biography | Opinion Piece |

Persuade - the author tries to get you to do something or believe them.

_____ _____

Inform - the author gives you information about a topic

_____ _____

Entertain - the author tells a story that the reader will enjoy through pictures or words.

_____ _____

Read a book that matches each of the author's purposes below. Write the title and explain why it matches the author's purpose.

Persuade: _____
(title)

_____

_____

Inform: _____
(title)

_____

_____

Entertain: _____
(title)

_____

_____

Read a book and write the lessons learned. Describe a time you learned a similar lesson (your connection)

My Book of Lessons Learned

By: _____

Lesson from your book:

_____

_____

_____

Your connection:

_____

_____

_____

School: _____

Teacher: _____

Date: _____

Read the short texts below. Tell the lesson learned.

1. Diego decided to stay up late on a school night to watch his favorite movie. The next day he found himself falling asleep. When he woke up, he figured out he missed the ending to the story being read aloud that he couldn't wait to hear. What lesson did Diego learn?

_____

_____

_____

1. Lisa's mom asked her to clean her room before her friends came over. Lisa decided to shove everything under her bed instead of putting things where they belong. When her friends came over, one of them reached for a game under the bed. Her friend saw the mess and Lisa became embarrassed. What lesson did Lisa learn?

_____

_____

_____

Read two books and write the lesson the character learned.

_____
Title of Book One

Lesson learned: _____

_____

_____

_____
Title of Book Two

Lesson learned: _____

_____

_____

GRADE 3
BOOKLET DIRECTIONS

My Second Book of Author's Purposes:
Students may need to be pre-taught on the ways authors write (persuade, inform, entertain, explain). Access to non-fiction/fiction examples of the author's purpose will be needed for this booklet.

My Book of Inferences:
Students will need to have access to fiction books.

My Next Book of Predictions:
Access to non-fiction books and coloring supplies will be needed for this booklet. Students may need review of text features and where to find them (table of contents, glossary, pictures and captions, graphs, and maps).

My Book of Evidence for Lessons Learned:
Students will need to have access to fiction books.

My Book of Character's Response to Challenges:
Students will need to have access to fiction books.

My Book of Character's Perspectives:
Students may need to be pre-taught perspectives and given examples. Access to a fiction book with more than one character's perspective and coloring supplies will be needed for this booklet.

My Book of Another's Opinions/Claims:
Students may need to be pre-taught opinions and claims. Access to a persuasive text will be needed for this booklet.

My Book of Literary Plots That are the Same and Different:
Students will need to have access to fiction books with similar plots with different cultural perspectives.

Some books we suggest:
Jumanji and _Zathura_ both by Chris Van Allberg
Wemberly Worried and _Chrysanthemum_ both by Kevin Henkes

My Book of Homophones:
Students may need to be pre-taught homophones.

Write to explain how to complete a certain task.
(example: build legos, make a recipe, draw something)

_____

_____

_____

_____

_____

_____

**My Second Book of
Author's Purpose**

By: _____

School: _____

Teacher: _____

Date: _____

Authors write for different purposes. You have learned they write to persuade, inform, and entertain.
In addition to these, authors can also write to explain.

Explain - the author gives the reader direction on how to do something.
(Example: Recipe, user manual)

List titles of texts that are examples of the author's purpose of explain:

_____

_____

_____

_____

Match each author's purpose to it's correct example. Some text examples could have more than one author's purpose.

A. Persuade   C. Inform

B. Entertain   D. Explain

Comic Strip _____   Commercial _____

Textbook _____   Instructions _____

Autobiography _____   Speech _____

Jokes _____   Poems _____

Write a story with a problem and solution. Make sure to include enough details to help the reader make an inference as to how the problem will be solved.

_____

_____

_____

_____

_____

_____

_____

My Book of Inferences

By: _____

School: _____

Teacher: _____

Date: _____

An inference is to make an educated guess.
Read two books. First, identify the problem and then make an inference as to what the solution will be.
Then, write the actual solution. Give yourself a star if your inference was correct.

_____
Title of Book 1

Problem:

_____

_____

Inference:

_____

_____

Continue Reading...
Solution:

_____

_____

_____
Title of Book 2

Problem:

_____

_____

Inference:

_____

_____

Continue Reading...
Solution:

_____

_____

Pretend you are writing a book about your favorite memory. Create a graph, map, and picture to help the reader make predictions about your book.

My Next Book of Predictions

Graph: Map:

By: _____

Picture(s):

School: _____

Teacher: _____

Caption:

_____

Date: _____

Using a non-fiction book, find the following text features and make a prediction of what the book will be about. Remember as you look at text features your predictions should become more detailed.

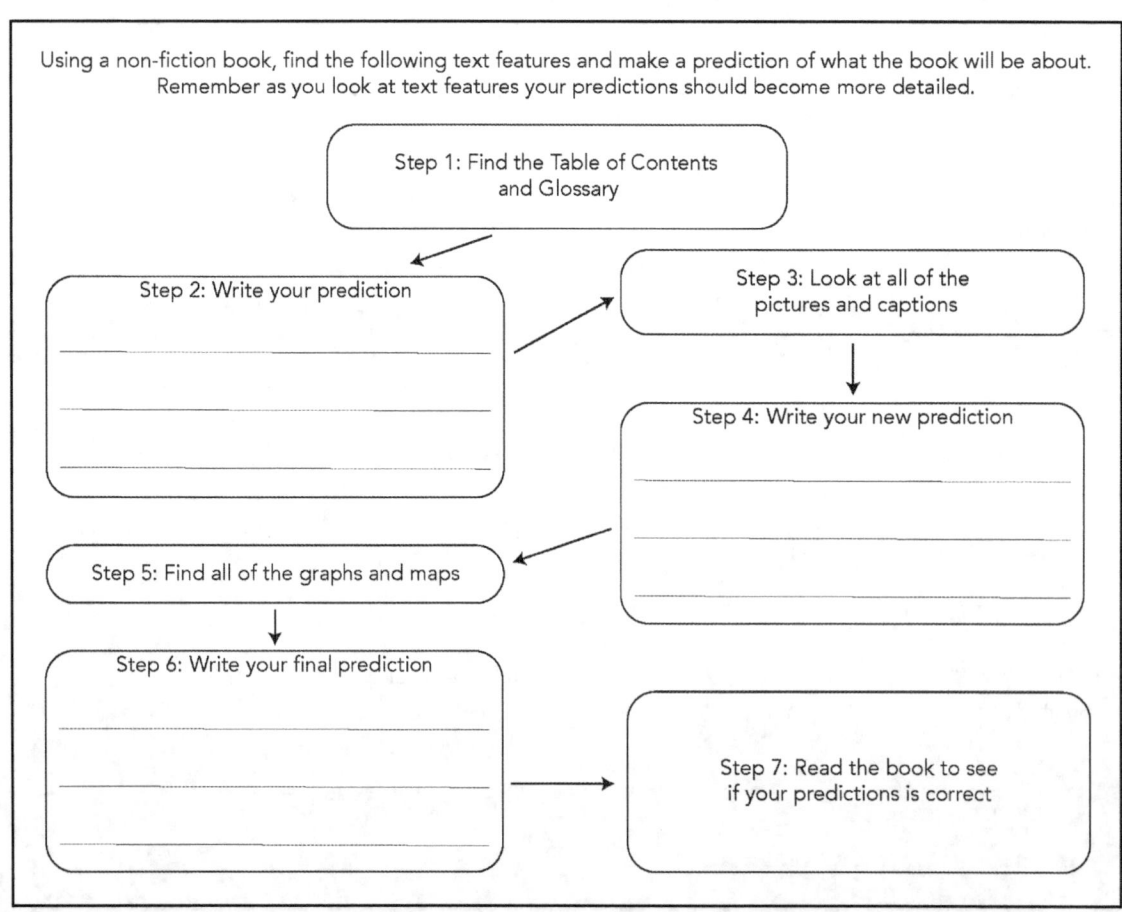

Step 1: Find the Table of Contents and Glossary

Step 2: Write your prediction

_____
_____
_____

Step 3: Look at all of the pictures and captions

Step 4: Write your new prediction

_____
_____
_____

Step 5: Find all of the graphs and maps

Step 6: Write your final prediction

_____
_____
_____

Step 7: Read the book to see if your predictions is correct

Student booklets are available via the QR code at the end of the book

Describe a time you watched someone learn a life lesson.	My Book of Evidence for Lessons Learned

By: _____

School: _____

Teacher: _____

Date: _____

Read two fiction books and provide evidence that leads up to the lesson each character learns.

_____
Title of Book 1

Evidence 1:

_____

_____

Evidence 2:

_____

_____

Lesson:

_____

_____

_____
Title of Book 2

Evidence 1:

_____

_____

Evidence 2:

_____

_____

Lesson:

_____

_____

Identify a time in your life when you were faced with a challenge. Describe how you responded to the challenge.

_____

_____

_____

_____

_____

_____

_____

My Book of Characters' Responses to Challenges

By: _____

School: _____

Teacher: _____

Date: _____

Read two fiction books and explain how the character in each book responded to the challenges they faced.

Title of Book One	Title of Book Two
Challenge 1:	Challenge 1:
Response 1:	Response 1:
Challenge 2:	Challenge 2:
Response 2:	Response 2:

Read a book with more than one character.
Draw a picture to show the two perspectives.

My Book of Character's Perspectives

By: _____

_____
Character's Name

School: _____

Teacher: _____

_____
Character's Name

Date: _____

Perspective - a character's attitude towards the world around them.

Read the short text and identify each character's perspective.

The Wildcats were on their way to the Championship basketball game. They rode the bus across town to face off their rivals, the Titans. In the bus, Katie was singing and dancing to the music hoping to make her teammates laugh. Annie sat quietly thinking, "I hope I don't make a mistake." As the bus screeched to a stop Annie wiped her sweating hands on her pants, while Katie yelled, "Let's go get 'em!"

Step 1: Underline evidence for Katie's perspective in blue.

Step 2: Underline evidence for Annie's perspective in red.

Step 3: Identify Katie's perspective
What is Katie's perspective?

_____
_____
_____

Step 4: Identify Annie's perspective
What is Annie's perspective?

_____
_____
_____

List your opinion on a certain topic.
Provide 2 claims to support your opinion.

Opinion:

_____

_____

_____

Supporting Claim:

_____

_____

_____

Supporting Claim:

_____

_____

_____

My Book of Another's Opinions/Claims

By: _____

School: _____

Teacher: _____

Date: _____

Opinion - a personal view or judgment made about someone or something that isn't always based on facts.

Claim - The evidence the writer uses to prove their opinion. The claim can be tested to be proved true or false.

Mark each statement below as either an opinion or claim:

I hate peas.
◊ Opinion   ◊ Claim

Dogs make great pets.
◊ Opinion   ◊ Claim

Every other girl in the school has a cell phone.
◊ Opinion   ◊ Claim

Mystery books are better than science fiction books.
◊ Opinion   ◊ Claim

50 percent of Americans have visited Disney World.
◊ Opinion   ◊ Claim

Read a persuasive text and identify the author's opinion along with their claim.

_____
Title

Opinion:

_____

_____

_____

Claim:

_____

_____

_____

Student booklets are available via the QR code at the end of the book

Write a story that has a plot with both similarities and differences to a favorite book.

_____

_____

_____

_____

_____

_____

_____

_____

My Book of Literary Plots That are the Same and Different

By: _____

School: _____

Teacher: _____

Date: _____

Read two fiction books that are similar. Then identify similarities and differences in their plots (characters, setting, conflict, resolution, and lesson learned).

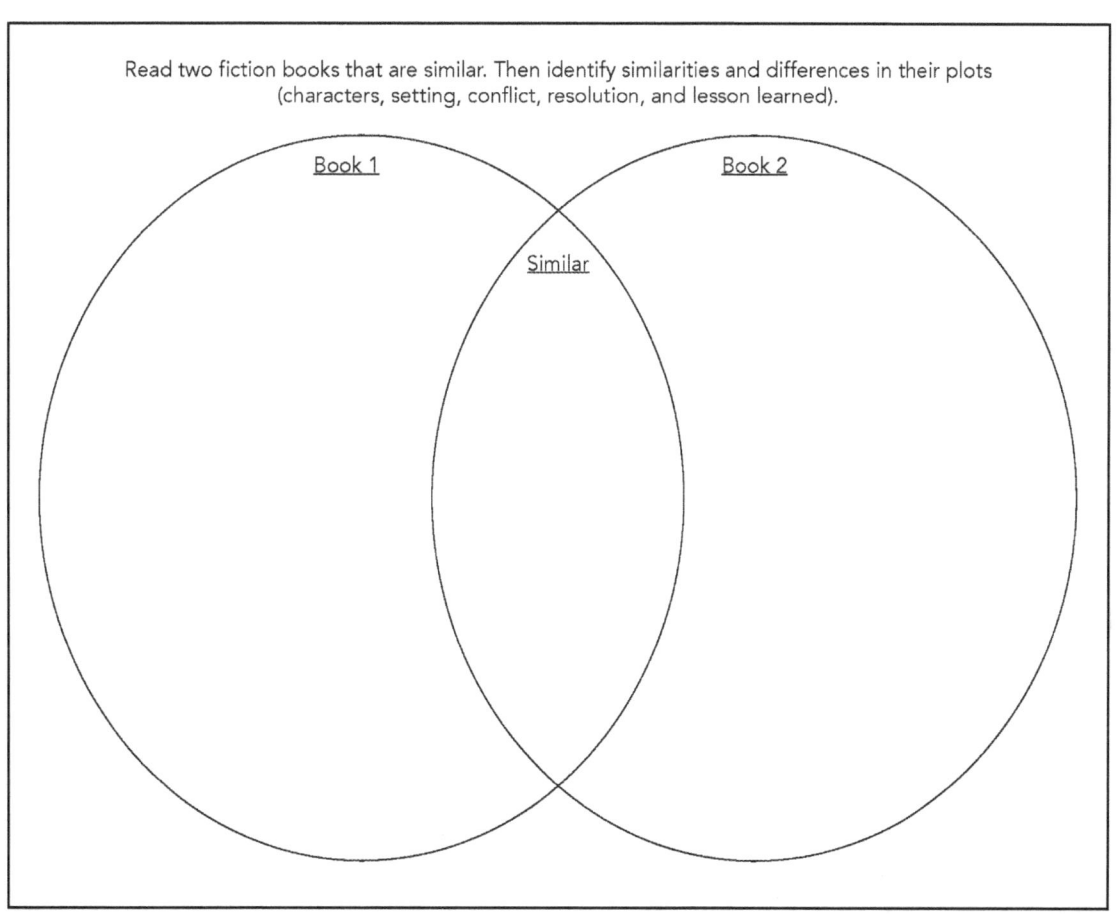

Book 1

Book 2

Similar

Write a homophone pair.
Draw a picture and write a sentence using both words.

My Book of Homophones

By: _____

_____   _____
Homophone 1   Homophone 2

School: _____

Teacher: _____

Date: _____

<u>Homophones</u> - words that sound the same, but have
different meaning or spelling.
(example: hair and hare)

Match the homophone pairs:

Wait   Whole

Write   To

Hole   Bare

Two   Weight

Bear   Right

Underline the homophone that is used incorrectly
in each sentence. Then rewrite the sentence using
the correct homophone.

I stubbed my tow.

_____

The prince gave the princess a rows.

_____

Maria eight a hotdog at the game.

_____

My mom sent me to the store to bye apples.

_____

I nailed down the bored.

_____

GRADE 4
BOOKLET DIRECTIONS

My Book of Similes and Metaphors:
Students may need to be pre-taught similes and metaphors. Access to texts with examples of similes and metaphors and coloring supplies will be needed for this booklet.

My Second Book of Prefixes and Suffixes:
Students may need to have access to books that contain prefixes and suffixes.

My Book of Homographs:
Students may need to be pre-taught homographs. Access to a non-fiction book and coloring supplies will be needed for this booklet.

My Book of Analyzing a Character:
Students may need to be pre-taught character traits. Access to a fiction book and coloring supplies will be needed for this booklet.

My Book of Comparing and Contrasting Literary Texts:
Students will need to have access to fiction books.

My Book of Summary and Theme:
Students will need to have access to books and coloring supplies.

My Book of Inferences Using Evidence:
Students will need to have access to books and coloring supplies.

My Book of Main Idea and Key Details:
Students may need to be pre-taught main idea and key details. Access to non-fiction books will be needed for this booklet.

My Book of Judging Actual Events:
Students will need to have access to a historical fiction and non-fiction book on the same topic.

My Book of Onomatopoeias:
Students may need to be pre-taught onomatopoeias. Access to a graphic novel or comic strip and coloring supplies will be needed for this booklet.

Choose a metaphor and simile from books you are reading or from the previous page and draw a picture and write what each example means.

My Book of Similes and Metaphors

By: _____

Simile

_____
_____
_____

Metaphor

_____
_____
_____

Either

_____
_____
_____

School: _____

Teacher: _____

Date: _____

Simile - a comparison of two things using the words "like" or "as".

Metaphor - a comparison of two things that does NOT use the words "like" or "as".

Read the sentences below and mark them as a smilie or a metaphor.

The classroom was a zoo.

◊ Simile   ◊ Metaphor

Her smile is like sunshine.

◊ Simile   ◊ Metaphor

He was as busy as a beaver.

◊ Simile   ◊ Metaphor

My computer is an old dinosaur.

◊ Simile   ◊ Metaphor

Alex's bedroom is as cold as ice.

◊ Simile   ◊ Metaphor

She is a night owl.

◊ Simile   ◊ Metaphor

Read books and list any examples of similes and metaphors.

Similes	Metaphors
_____	_____
_____	_____
_____	_____
_____	_____
_____	_____
_____	_____
_____	_____

Student booklets are available via the QR code at the end of the book

As you read, list words with the prefixes and suffixes you have learned in this booklet.

_____   _____

_____   _____

_____   _____

_____   _____

_____   _____

_____   _____

_____   _____

_____   _____

My Second Book of Prefixes and Suffixes

By: _____

School: _____

Teacher: _____

Date: _____

Use the definitions to fill in the correct prefix for each word.

<u>In- / Im-</u>: Not
<u>Anti</u>-: Against
<u>De</u>-: Remove
<u>Dis</u>-: Not

_____agree   _____social

_____rail   _____possible

_____slavery   _____compose

_____obey   _____flate

_____able   _____honest

Rewrite each word using the correct suffix. Remember some base words may need to be changed.

<u>-ly</u>: Characteristic of
       Adding -ly changes an adjective to an adverb
<u>-able /-ible</u>: can be done
<u>-ment</u>: action or process
<u>-ful</u>: full of

_____   _____
(reverse)   (slow)

_____   _____
(change)   (amaze)

_____   _____
(lone)   (pain)

_____   _____
(wonder)   (sink)

_____   _____
(disappoint)   (discuss)

Write a homograph pair.
Draw a picture and write a sentence using both words.

My Book of Homographs

By: _____

_____ _____
Homograph 1   Homograph 2

School: _____

Teacher: _____

Date: _____

Homographs - words that are spelled the same but have different pronunciations and meanings.
Example: Tear (cry) and Tear (rip)

Draw pictures and write sentences using the two meanings of the homograph below:

BOW

Write a sentence for each homograph to show both meanings.

Bass
Sentence 1:
_____
_____

Sentence 2:
_____
_____

Close
Sentence 1:
_____
_____

Sentence 2:
_____
_____

Student booklets are available via the QR code at the end of the book

List traits of a person in your life. Provide evidence (words, actions) to support their traits.

My Book of Analyzing a Character

By: _____

_____
Name

Words:

Actions:

Traits with Evidence:

_____

_____

_____

_____

School: _____

Teacher: _____

Date: _____

Read a fictional story and collect evidence to identify the character's strongest traits.

Thoughts:

Words:

Actions:

Using the evidence on the previous page, list as many character traits that apply to the character using complete sentences.
Give the best evidence for each character unit.

_____

_____

_____

_____

_____

_____

_____

_____

_____

_____

_____

Write a story that has both similar and different literary elements as your favorite tall tale.

_____
_____
_____
_____
_____
_____
_____
_____
_____
_____

My Book of Comparing and Contrasting Literary Text

By: _____

School: _____

Teacher: _____

Date: _____

Read two fiction books and compare and contrast the literary elements (characters, setting, conflict, plot, and theme)

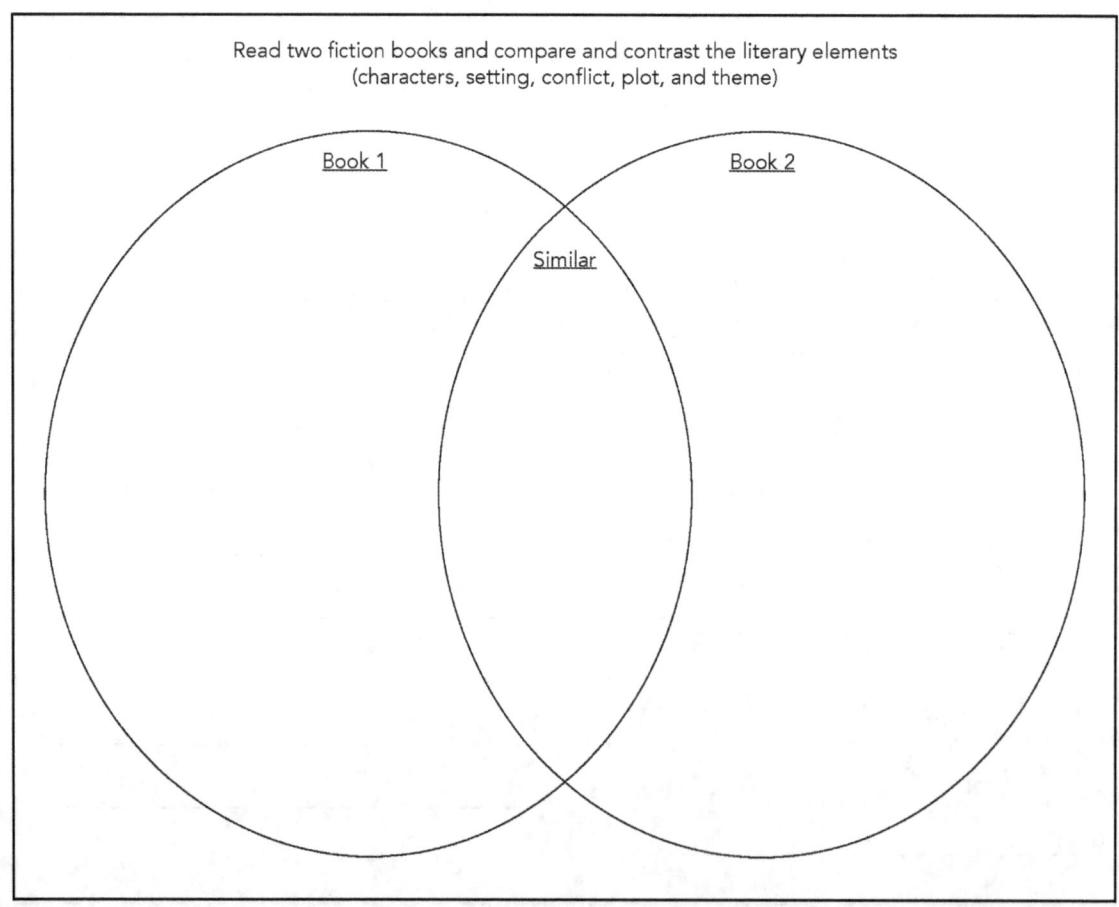

Book 1   Similar   Book 2

Student booklets are available via the QR code at the end of the book

Write a story that has both similarities and differences in its summary and theme as a favorite book.

My Book of Summary and Theme

By: _____

_____
_____
_____
_____
_____
_____
_____
_____
_____

School: _____

Teacher: _____

Date: _____

Summary - retells the main events of a story in a shorter version.

Theme - a message or lesson from the story that you can apply to your own life.

Read a fictional book. Write a summary using the chart below. Then complete the theme.

Somebody	Wanted	But	So	Then

The theme of the story is...

_____
_____
_____

Student booklets are available via the QR code at the end of the book

Create a series of pictures to tell a story. Be sure the pictures have enough detail for the reader to identify the problem and solution.

My Book of Inferences Using Evidence

By: _____

School: _____

Teacher: _____

Date: _____

Read two fiction books and explain how the character in each book responded to the challenges they faced.

Title of Book 1	Title of Book 2
Inference:	Inference:
Evidence:	Evidence:
Inference:	Inference:
Evidence:	Evidence:

Student booklets are available via the QR code at the end of the book

Pretend you are writing a book about your life thus far. Provide the main idea and key details that would best describe your life.

My Book of Main Idea and Key Details

By: _____

Main Idea:

_____

_____

_____

_____

Key Details:

1. _____

_____

2. _____

_____

3. _____

_____

School: _____

Teacher: _____

Date: _____

Main Idea - What the text is mostly about.

Key Detail - Facts or examples that tell more about the main idea.

Read two fiction books and explain how the character in each book responded to the challenges they faced.

Title of Book 1

Main Idea:

_____

_____

_____

Key Details:

1. _____

2. _____

3. _____

Title of Book 2

Main Idea:

_____

_____

_____

Key Details:

1. _____

2. _____

3. _____

Read a non-fiction book and collect facts about the topic. Once you have collected the facts, write a literary story with related events/facts.

My Book of Judging Actual Events

By: _____

School: _____

Teacher: _____

Date: _____

Read a literary and a non-fiction book on the same topic. In the chart below, fill in events/facts as you read. Once you are done reading, cross out any **literary** events/facts that were not repeated in the non-fiction book.

Literary Book Title	Non-Fiction Book Title

Student booklets are available via the QR code at the end of the book

Tell a story using a comic strip.
Make sure to include several onomatopoeias.

My Book of Onomatopoeias

By: _____

School: _____

Teacher: _____

Date: _____

Onomatopoeia - words that sound like the object they name or the sound those objects make.

Read a graphic novel or comic strip and list the onomatopoeias you find:

Circle the words that are examples of onomatopoeias:

Firework	Hee - Haw
Zipper	Snake
Choo Choo	Chomp
Pound	Boom
Slurp	Fan
Pow	Drop

GRADE 5
BOOKLET DIRECTIONS

My Book of Homonyms:
Students may need to be pre-taught homonyms. Access to coloring supplies will be needed for this booklet.

My Book of Comparing and Contrasting Settings:
Students will need to have access to a literary book that contains flashbacks or flash forwards that change the time period or place.

My Book of Connecting Themes to Real Events:
Students will need to have access to two literary books.

Detective: What Does This Author Really Think?
Students will need to have access to two opinion texts (current event articles, blog posts, comic strips, etc.).

My Second Book of Judging Actual Events:
Students will need to have access to a historical fiction and non-fiction book on the same topic and coloring supplies for this booklet.

My Book of Latin Roots:
Students may need to be pre-taught root words and given examples.

My Book of Alliteration:
Students may need to be pre-taught alliteration and given examples. Access to a variety of text such as: articles, song lyrics, comic books and coloring supplies will be needed for this booklet.

My Book of Personification:
Students may need to be pre-taught personification and given examples. Access to coloring supplies will be needed for this booklet.

My Book of Idioms:
Students may need to be pre-taught idioms and given examples. Access to a variety of text such as: articles, song lyrics, comic books and coloring supplies will be needed for this booklet.

My Book of Hyperboles:
Students may need to be pre-taught hyperbole and given examples.

Create silly sentences using homonym pairs in each sentence:

_____

_____

_____

_____

_____

_____

_____

_____

_____

_____

My Book of Homonyms

By: _____

School: _____

Teacher: _____

Date: _____

Homonyms - two or more words with the **same spelling and pronunciation** but **different meanings.**
Example: Tie - to band together, Tie - article of clothing worn around the neck.

Draw a picture for each homonym pair to show the two different meanings.

Fall

Rose

Write a sentence for each homonym to show both meanings:

Quarter
Sentence 1:

_____

Sentence 2:

_____

Bank
Sentence 1:

_____

Sentence 2:

_____

Student booklets are available via the QR code at the end of the book

Write a story with the same setting (time and place) but a different plot as your most recent read.

_____

_____

_____

_____

_____

_____

_____

_____

_____

_____

My Book of Comparing and Contrasting Setting

By: _____

School: _____

Teacher: _____

Date: _____

Read a fictional book and compare and contrast the setting (time period and place) within the book.

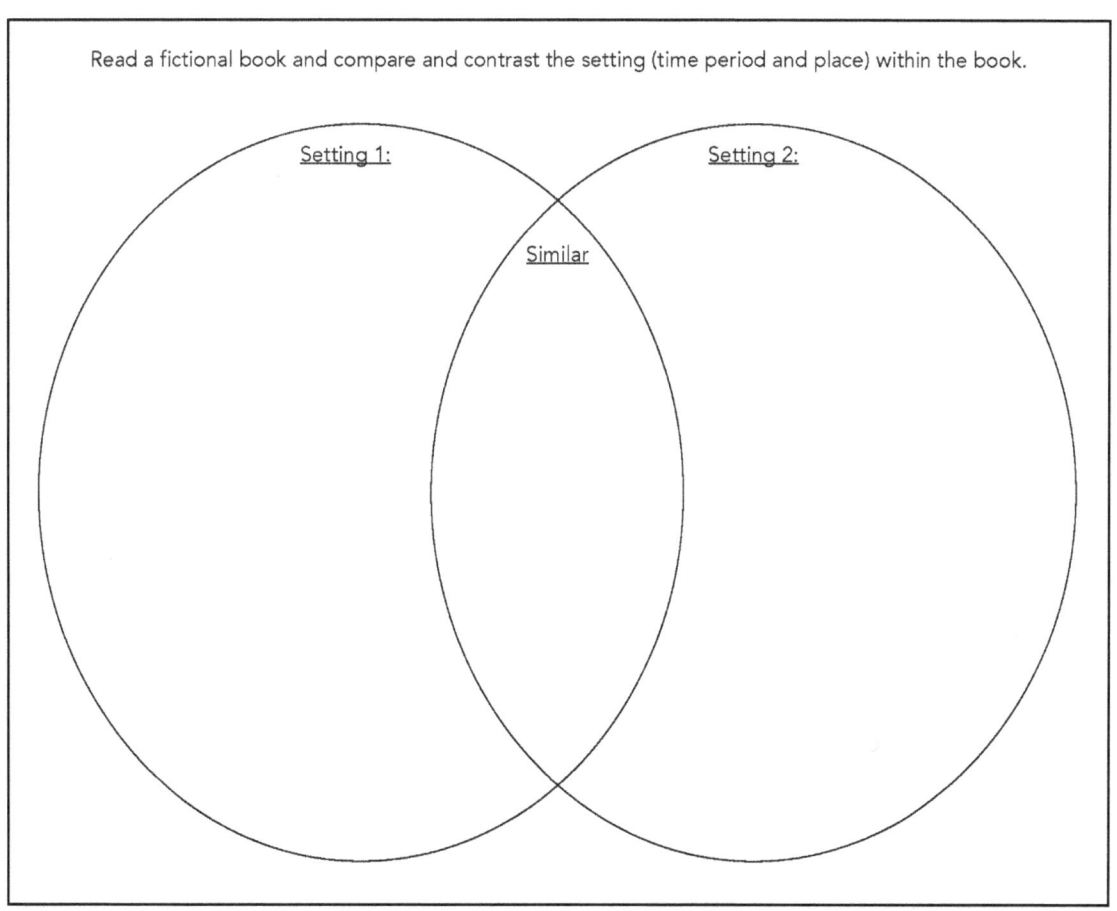

Setting 1:

Setting 2:

Similar

Write a realistic fiction story that has the same theme as one of the books you've read:

_____

_____

_____

_____

_____

_____

_____

_____

_____

_____

My Book of Connecting Themes to Real Events

By: _____

School: _____

Teacher: _____

Date: _____

Read two fictional books and identify their theme. Then write about a time when you have experienced each theme in your life.

_____
Title of Book 1

Theme:

_____

_____

_____

Real-World Connection:

_____

_____

_____

_____
Title of Book 2

Theme:

_____

_____

_____

Real-World Connection:

_____

_____

_____

Student booklets are available via the QR code at the end of the book

After reading both opinion texts, which text do you side with? Explain why.

Detective: What Does This Author Really Think?

By: _____

School: _____

Teacher: _____

Date: _____

Read two opinion texts that have different perspectives on the same topic. While reading, write down the author's belief and evidence that supports their opinion.

_____
Title of Text 1

Author's Belief:

_____

_____

_____

Evidence:

_____

_____

_____

Title of Text 2

Author's Belief:

_____

_____

_____

Evidence:

_____

_____

_____

Student booklets are available via the QR code at the end of the book

Research an important event in American history, Create a book cover representing the details of the historical event.

My Second Book of Judging Actual Events

By: ____________________

School: ____________________

Teacher: ____________________

Date: ____________________

Read a literary and a non-fiction book on the same topic. In the chart below, fill in events/facts as you read. Once you are done reading cross out any literary events/facts that were not repeated in the non-fiction book.

Literary Book Title	Non-Fiction Book Title

Student booklets are available via the QR code at the end of the book

Research more Latin roots. Then choose one to create a diagram that displays the root word with all the possible prefixes and suffixes that can be applied.

My Book of Latin Roots

By: _____

School: _____

Teacher: _____

Date: _____

Latin Roots - a word with a Latin origin that does not have a prefix or suffix, but one can be added to change the meaning of the word.
Example: root - audi, audience

Match the following Latin roots with their meanings

Form
(transform format)   A. to draw or pull

Tract
(attract, subtract)   B. to look

Spect
(inspect, spectator)   C. to shape

Act
(action, actor)   D. to act or do

List as many related words as you can find for each Latin root:

port	ject
dict	pend

Create and illustrate two silly alliterations:

My Book of Alliterations

By: _____

School: _____

Teacher: _____

Date: _____

Alliteration - the repetition of the same sound at the beginning of a sequence of words.
Example: **C**indy **S**wam in the **S**wimming Pool.

Read each sentence and underline the words that create an alliteration:

1. Mary made mouth-watering muffins on Monday.

2. Andrea ate apples all day.

3. Soft snow falls silently.

4. The tornado tossed the turtle into the tree.

Read a variety of text (song lyrics, articles, comic books, etc.) and list as many examples of alliterations as you can find.

Text	Alliteration
_____	_____
_____	_____
_____	_____
_____	_____
_____	_____
_____	_____
_____	_____
_____	_____
_____	_____

Choose or create a personification and draw both the literal and figurative meanings

My Book of Personification

By: _____

School: _____

Teacher: _____

Date: _____

Personification - giving human qualities to animals or objects.

Read each sentence and underline the word or phrase that personifies the animal or objects.
Example: The **stars winked** at me.

1. The last piece of cake was calling my name.

2. The plant was begging for water.

3. The wind whistled through the trees.

4. Lighting danced across the sky.

Add a phrase to the objects below that best personifies them.

The sun _____

_____

My alarm clock _____

_____

The thunder _____

_____

Her balloon _____

_____

My Book of Idioms

Idioms are often used to describe real-life situations. Research the meaning of the following three idioms:
"don't judge a book by its cover"
"Rome wasn't built in a day"
"the end doesn't justify the means"
Then choose one of those idioms to write about a real-world connection you've experienced.

_____

_____

_____

_____

_____

_____

_____

_____

_____

By: _____

School: _____

Teacher: _____

Date: _____

Idiom - a phrase that means something different from its literal meaning.
Example: Easy does it = slow down

For each idiom, draw pictures that show the literal meaning and the figurative meaning.

All in the same boat.

Letting the cat out of the bag.

Read a variety of texts (song lyrics, articles, comic books, etc.) to find multiple idioms. List them in the chart below and state their figurative meaning.

Idiom	Figurative Meaning

Write a poem using multiple examples of hyperboles.

My Book of Hyperboles

By: _____

School: _____

Teacher: _____

Date: _____

Hyperbole - an exaggerated statement.
Example: Dying of laughter.

Match each phrase with its corresponding hyperbole:

The man was so hungry he could...   A. a mile wide

Her smile was...   B. as a toothpick

I am so confused my head...   C. sleep for a year

He is as skinny...   D. eat a horse

She was so tired she could...   E. is spinning

Replace the words in parenthesis with a hyperbole
Write the new sentence on the line below.

I have (a lot) of things to do today.

_____

My dog is (large).

_____

His homework took (a long time) to complete.

_____

It is raining (hard).

_____

GRADE 6
BOOKLET DIRECTIONS

My Book of Greek Roots:
Students may need to be pre-taught root words and given examples.

My Book of Inferential Questions:
Students will need access to a literary chapter book of their choosing.

My Book of Breaking Down a Plot to Identify Theme:
Students will need access to a literary chapter book of their choosing.

My Book of Multicultural Perspectives:
Students will need access to a historical fiction book with multiple cultural perspectives.

Some books we suggest:
Refugee by Alan Gratz
Ground Zero by Alan Gratz
Towers Falling by Jewell Parker Rhodes

My Book of Central Ideas:
Students may need to be pre-taught central idea. Central idea is the secondary level term for main idea. The students will have prior knowledge of main idea from previous booklets. Access to a non-fiction book and coloring supplies will be needed for this booklet.

My Book of Arguments:
Students will need access to an opinion article on a topic of their choosing.

My Book of Allusions:
Students may need to be taught beforehand about allusion and given examples.

My Book of Puns:
Students may need to be pre-taught puns and given examples. A variety of text such as: articles, song lyrics, comic books will be needed for this booklet.

My Book of Symbolism:
Students may need to be pre-taught symbolism and given examples. Access to their favorite animated movie and coloring supplies will be needed for this booklet.

' Research more Greek roots. Then choose one to create a diagram that displays the root word with all the possible prefixes and suffixes that can be applied.

My Book of Greek Roots

By: _____

School: _____

Teacher: _____

Date: _____

Greek Roots - a word with a Greek origin that does not have a prefix or suffix, but one can be added to change the meaning of the word.
Example: root - **biblio**, **biblio**graphy

Match the following Greek roots with their meanings

Auto (autobiography, automatic)	A. Life
Bio (biography, biology)	B. Water
Meter (thermometer, speedometer)	C. People
Dem (democracy, demographics)	D. Write
Hydro (hydrant, hydroflask)	E. Self
Graph (autography, calligraphy)	F. Measure

List as many related words as you can find for each Greek root:

dec	gram
phon	**micro**

Write an interview for a character of a book you've read. Ask multiple inferential questions and answer these questions as to how you think the character would respond.

_____

_____

_____

_____

_____

_____

_____

_____

_____

My Book of Inferential Questions

By: _____

School: _____

Teacher: _____

Date: _____

Inferential Questions - questions whose answers are not found directly in the text. To answer these questions, the reader has to look for clues in the text and connect them with what they already know in order to figure out what the author is saying.

Read a chapter book and after every few chapters, stop to write and answer inferential questions.

_____
Book Title

Chapter	Inferential Question(s)	Answer(s)

Student booklets are available via the QR code at the end of the book

Pick two of your favorite songs. Use the lyrics to help you identify the implied themes.

My Book of Breaking Down a Plot to Identify Theme

By: _____

_____
First Song Title

Implied Theme:

_____

_____

_____

_____
Second Song Title

Implied Theme:

_____

_____

_____

School: _____

Teacher: _____

Date: _____

Read a literary book and complete the plot diagram below describing the important details. Be sure to label the elements of plot. Then use the completed plot diagram to help you identify the implied theme of the story.

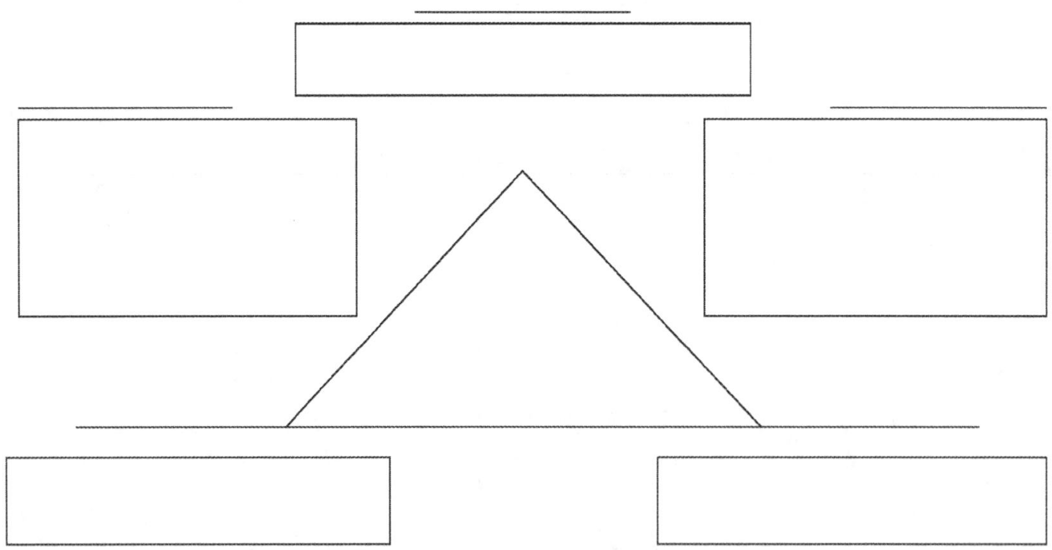

In this story, the implied theme is _____

_____

_____

Student booklets are available via the QR code at the end of the book

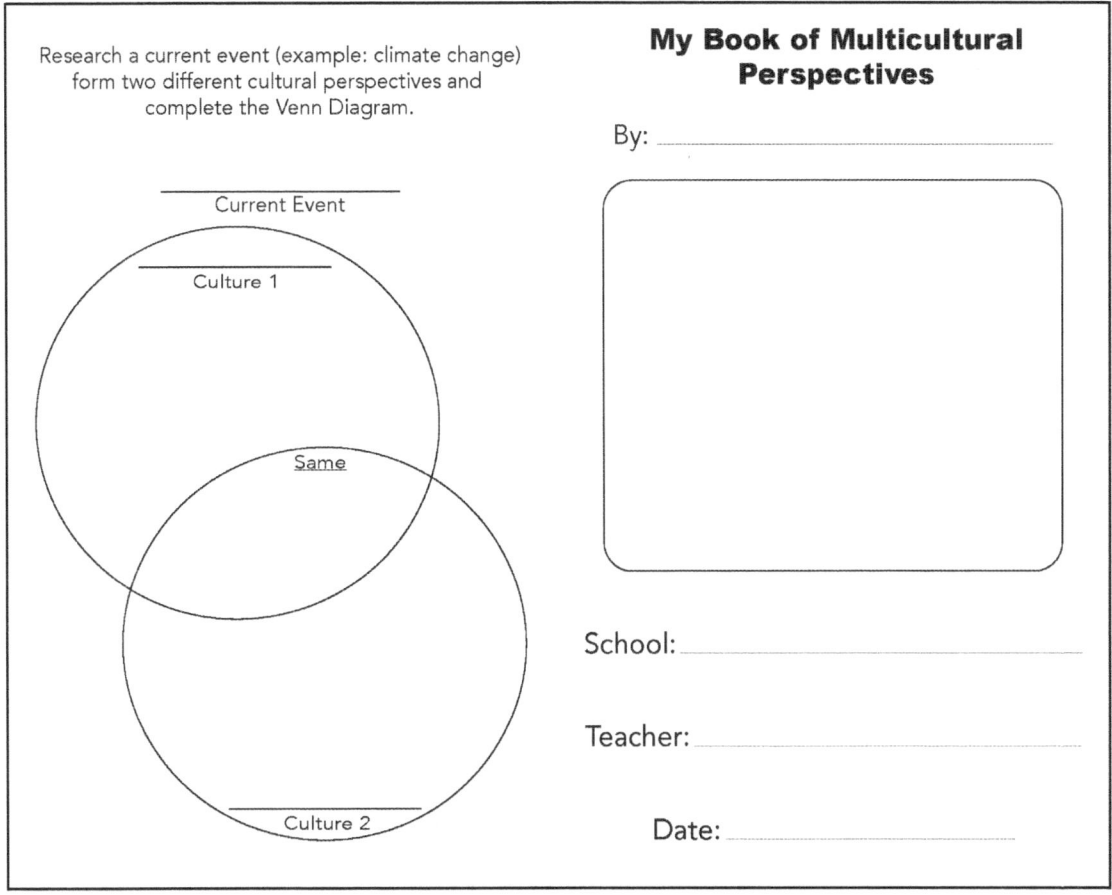

Research a current event (example: climate change) form two different cultural perspectives and complete the Venn Diagram.

_____
Current Event

_____
Culture 1

Same

_____
Culture 2

My Book of Multicultural Perspectives

By: _____

School: _____

Teacher: _____

Date: _____

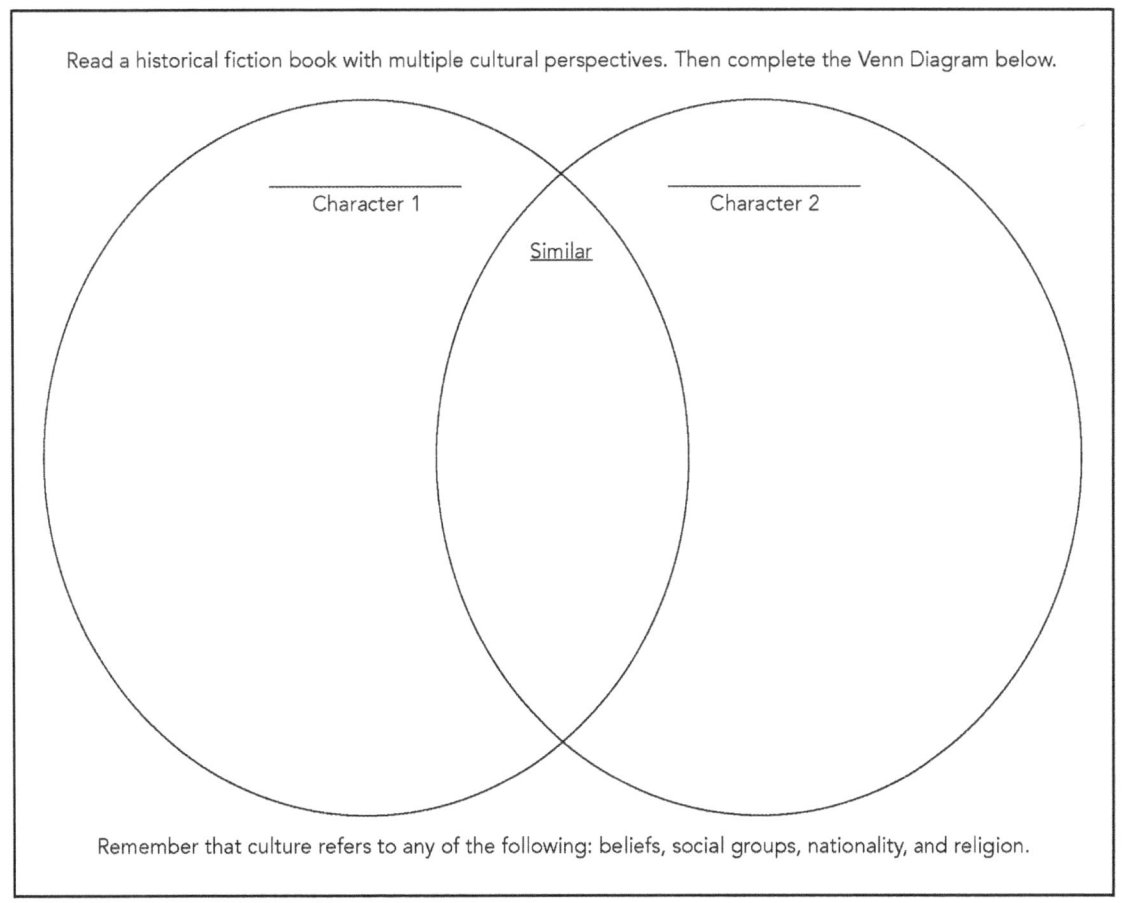

Read a historical fiction book with multiple cultural perspectives. Then complete the Venn Diagram below.

_____
Character 1

Similar

_____
Character 2

Remember that culture refers to any of the following: beliefs, social groups, nationality, and religion.

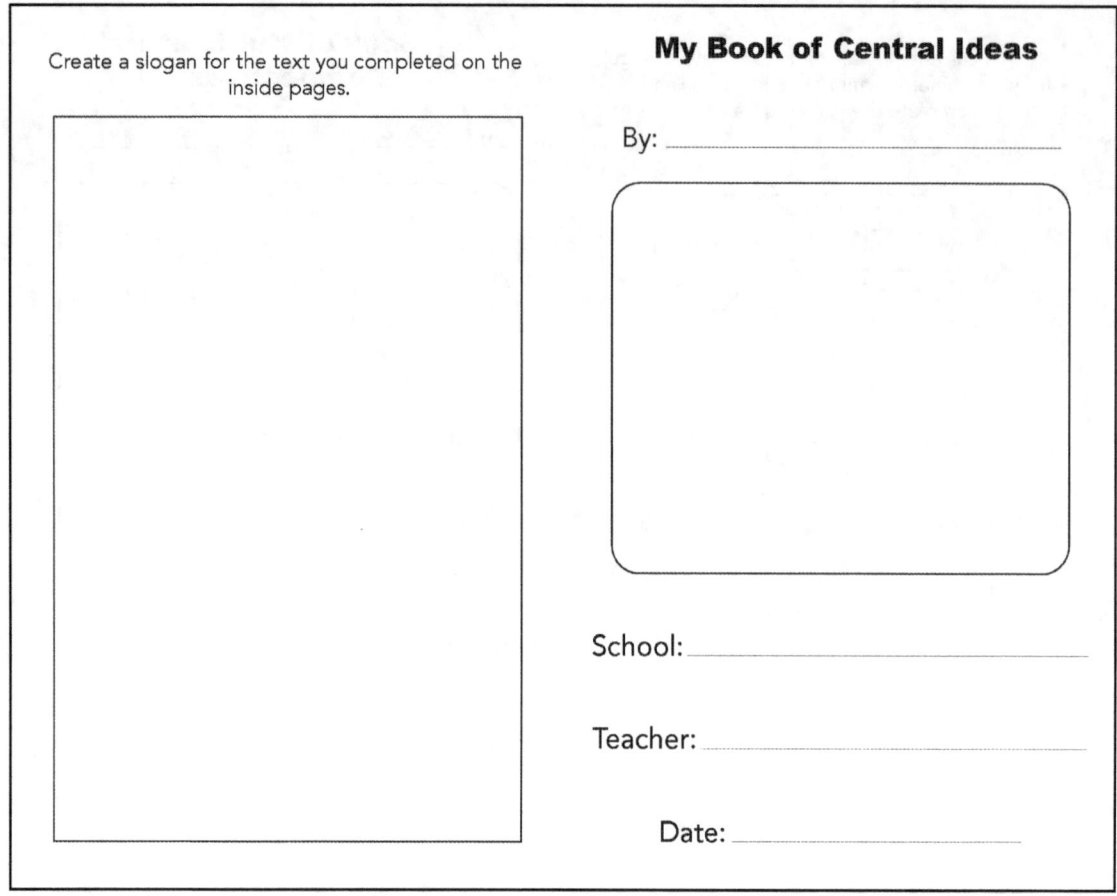

Create a slogan for the text you completed on the inside pages.

My Book of Central Ideas

By: _____

School: _____

Teacher: _____

Date: _____

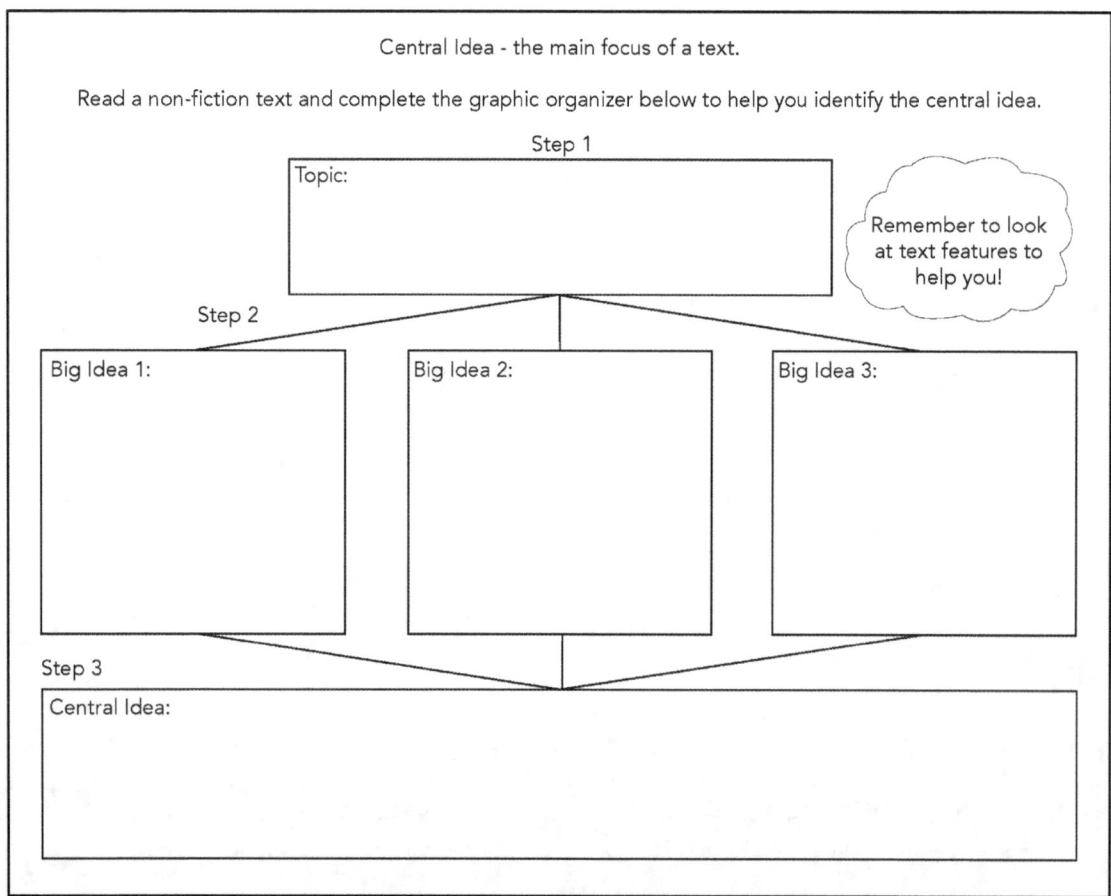

Central Idea - the main focus of a text.

Read a non-fiction text and complete the graphic organizer below to help you identify the central idea.

Step 1

Topic:

Remember to look at text features to help you!

Step 2

Big Idea 1:

Big Idea 2:

Big Idea 3:

Step 3

Central Idea:

Student booklets are available via the QR code at the end of the book

Create your own argument on a current topic

My Book of Arguments

_____
Topic

By: _____

My opinion:

_____
_____
_____

Biases	Actual Facts

School: _____

Teacher: _____

Date: _____

Bias - to favor some ideas or people over others.

Read an opinion article on a topic of your choice, Complete the chart below to show how the author defends their opinions by using actual facts and biases for their overall argument.

_____
Topic

Author's opinion:

_____
_____

Biases	Actual Facts

Create multiple allusions of your own:

My Book of Allusions

By: _____

School: _____

Teacher: _____

Date: _____

Allusion - a reference within a literary text to a person, place, event, or to another work of literature.
Example: Peanut butter is my "achilles heel". The term "achilles heel" comes from Greek mythology meaning something's weakness.

Read the following statements and identify what it's alluding to:

She felt like she had won a golden ticket.

_____

He's a real Einstein.

_____

Sally told her crying sister to let it go.

_____

If I'm not home by midnight, my car will turn into a pumpkin.

_____

A lot of allusions come from Greek mythology. Research these modern day allusions and list their connections below.

Modern Day	Greek Mythology
_____	_____
_____	_____
_____	_____
_____	_____
_____	_____
_____	_____
_____	_____
_____	_____

Create multiple puns of your own.

My Book of Puns

By: _____

_____

_____

_____

_____

_____

_____

_____

_____

_____

School: _____

Teacher: _____

Date: _____

Puns - a play on words, that is used as a comical relief within a text.
Example: I'm so **board** I really wish something fun **wood** come along.

Read each pun and underline the word(s) or phrase(s) that represents play on word. Then read it to a family member and see if they get it.

1. Past, present, and future walked into the room. It was tense.

2. I work as a baker because I knead dough.

3. To write with a broken pencil is pointless.

4. I couldn't figure out how to buckle my seatbelt. Then it clicked!

Find puns within a variety of text (songs, comic strips, graphic novels, etc.) and copy them down.

Text	Pun

Draw a picture with multiple symbols that represent your life.

My Book of Symbolism

By: _____

School: _____

Teacher: _____

Date: _____

<u>Symbolism</u> - when a word is used to mean or represent something other than its typical definition, to help authors communicate their messages to readers.
Example: **Rose** is often used to represent **love**.

Match each example of symbolism to what it represents:

Four Leaf Clover   A. Luck

Broken Mirror   B. Doom

Dove   C. Evilness

Snake   D. Life or Purity

Dark Clouds   E. Bad Luck

Watch your favorite animated movie and try to identify the hidden symbols within the movie.

_____
Movie Title

<u>Symbolism</u> | <u>Represents</u>

CONTINUE CREATING LITERARY EXPERTS

BONUS BOOKLETS

A quick internet search for literary terms brings up hundreds of words. In addition, there are many topics to study as students gain more meaning from language and increase their writing skills.

Thus, the following blank pages are designed for students to write additional booklets about literary terms not included in *How to Create Language Experts with Literary Terms*. After selecting a new term, students select the format that best fits the task of writing about the literary term or concept.

There are times when children become so engrossed with a particular term that they want to make their booklet larger. These blank pages can also be used to add to existing booklets included in *How to Create Language Experts with Literary Terms*.

Student booklets are available via the QR code at the end of the book

My Book of _____

By: _____

School: _____

Teacher: _____

Date: _____

_____
Title of Book 1

_____
Title of Book 2

Student booklets are available via the QR code at the end of the book

My art:

Student booklets are available via the QR code at the end of the book

Book 1 Title: _____   Book 2 Title: _____

Book Title

Book Title

Student booklets are available via the QR code at the end of the book

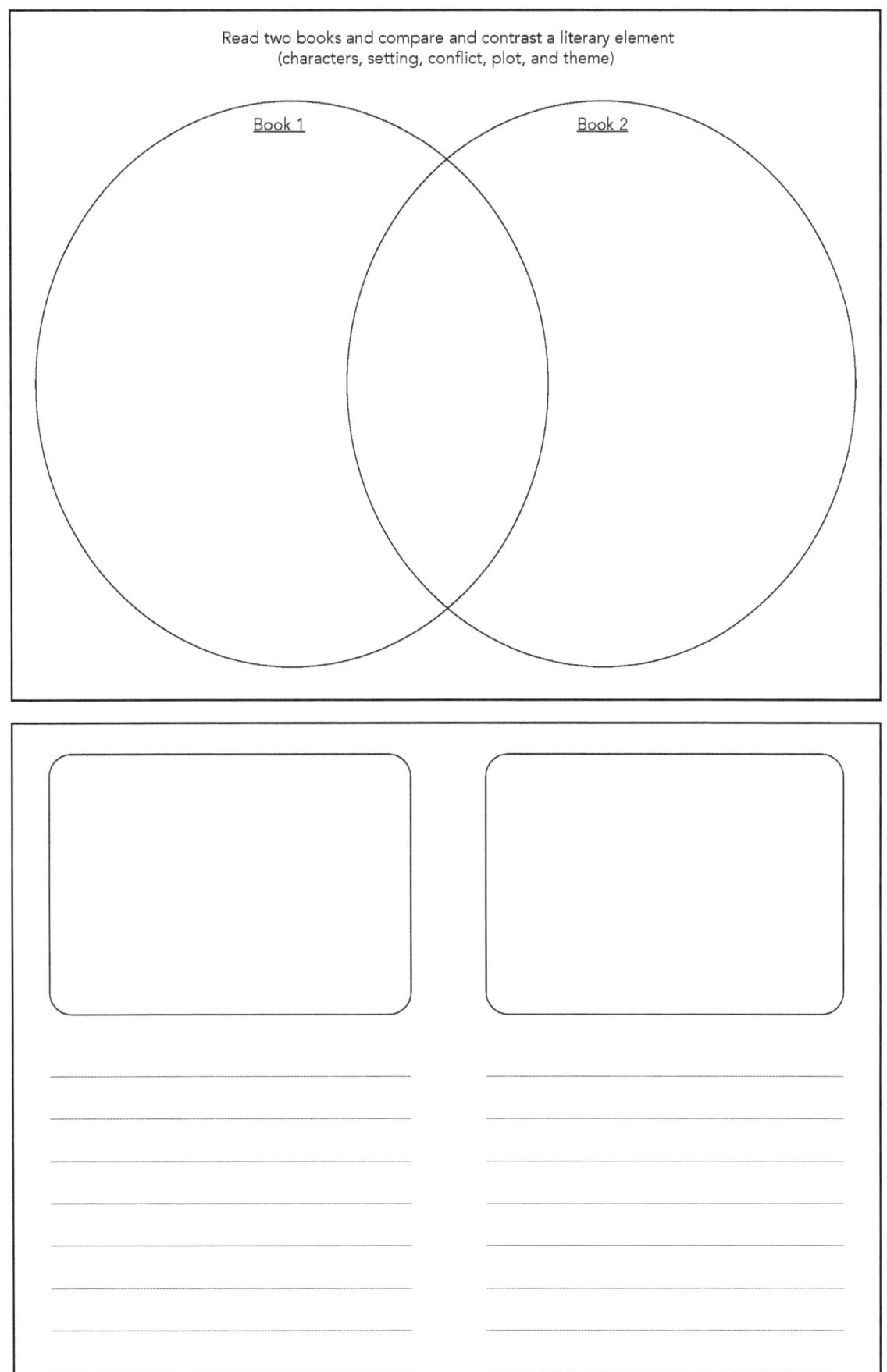

Read two books and compare and contrast a literary element
(characters, setting, conflict, plot, and theme)

Book 1   Book 2

Student booklets are available via the QR code at the end of the book

---

<u>   </u>
Book Title

<u>   </u>
Book Title

<u>   </u>
Title of Book One

<u>   </u>
Title of Book Two

Student booklets are available via the QR code at the end of the book

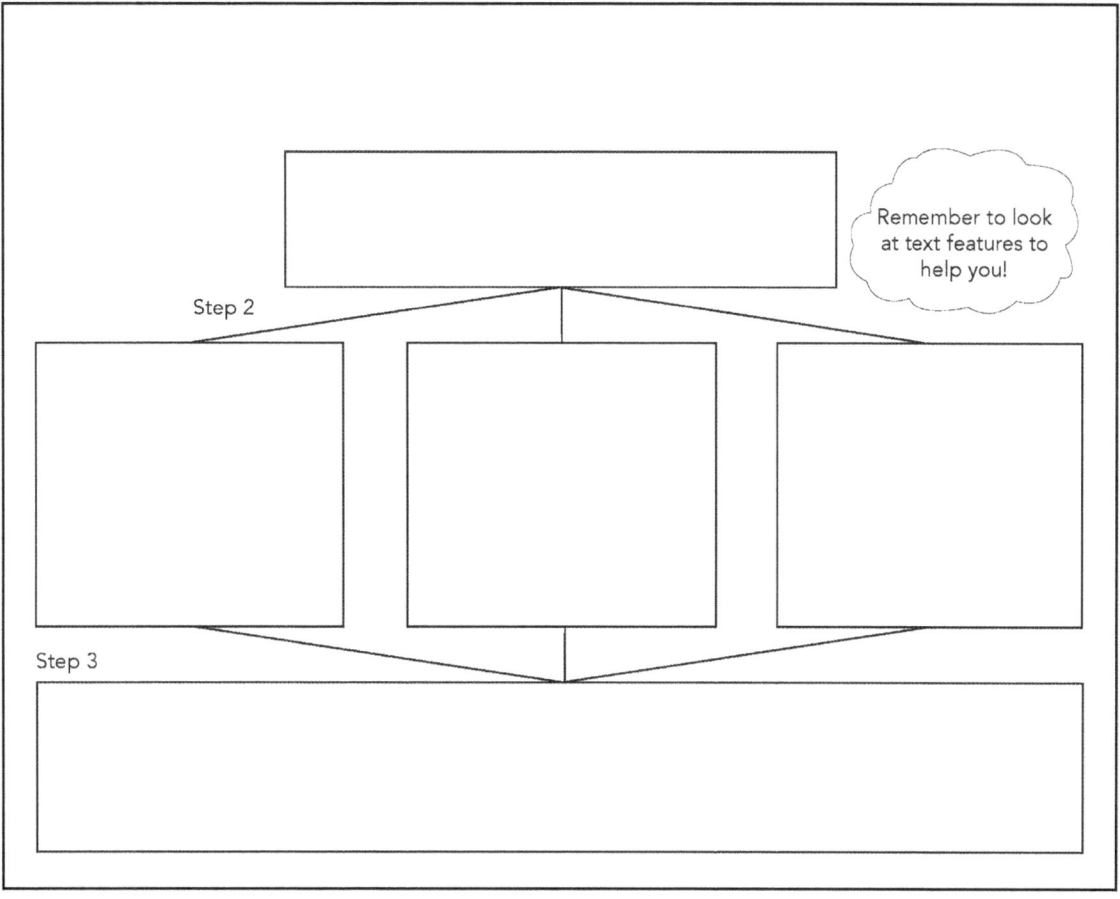

Step 2

Remember to look at text features to help you!

Step 3

STUDENT BOOKLET
DOWNLOAD

Purchasers of **How to Create Language Experts with Literary Terms** may use this QR code to download booklets from this book at no extra cost. This will ease the process of making copies for students and expand learning options. Both the print and digital download versions of this material are protected by copyright laws.

QR codes can be found in all LtoJ books, providing access to digital downloads of student worksheets.

ABOUT THE AUTHORS

Codi Hrouda grew up in the small town of Hubbard, Nebraska. After completing high school, Codi went on to pursue her degree in Elementary Education at Wayne State College, and graduated with a BA in Elementary Education in 2000.

Once graduated, Codi accepted her first job at Thurston Elementary School, in Thurston, Nebraska, as a fifth and sixth grade combination teacher. A year later, she and her husband moved to Columbus, Nebraska where she taught a year of first grade and then thirteen years of fourth grade at Centennial Elementary School. While teaching full-time in Columbus, she completed her master's degree in Curriculum and Instruction through Wayne State College. She graduated with her master's degree in May of 2006.

In 2014, Codi and her husband moved their family back to the area where she grew up to raise their three daughters. Codi accepted a fifth grade position at Dakota City Elementary in Dakota City, Nebraska where she continues to teach today. She just completed her twenty-second year of teaching in 2022. Codi spends her free time attending her daughters' activities, decorating, reading, and spending time with her family and friends.

Emma McInerney grew up in the small town of Elk Point, South Dakota. After completing high school, Emma went on to pursue a degree in healthcare at South Dakota State University (SDSU).

In 2015, she realized she was ready for a career change because her passion lies in education. She transferred to Dakota State University (DSU), earned a degree in Elementary Education, and graduated in 2019. Emma began her first job at Dakota City Elementary, in Dakota City, Nebraska, as a fifth grade teacher. While teaching full-time she completed her Masters degree in Curriculum and Instruction through Wayne State College, graduating in May of 2022. Emma concluded her third year of teaching in 2022, and she continues to teach alongside her co-author, Codi Hrouda.

Emma returned to her hometown of Elk Point after graduating, and spends her free time reading, gardening, and spending time with her boyfriend, family, and friends.

Dr. Lyle Lee Jenkins is an author, speaker, and recognized authority in improving educational outcomes. He believes that implementing a growth mindset and celebrating progress are the keys to helping students learn more and retain their enthusiasm for school.

His education experience, that spans over 50 years, ranges from working as a teacher, a principal, and a school superintendent in the California School System to being a University Professor. In 2003, Lyle Lee founded LtoJ, LLC hoping to impact and guide the way we approach education.

Lyle Lee Jenkins has authored six books showcasing continuous improvement in schools, including *How to Create a Perfect School, Optimize Your School, Permission to Forget, From Systems Thinking to Systemic Action, Improving Student Learning,* and *How to Create a Perfect Home School.* All literature offers powerful, practical suggestions for every aspect of education. The two most influential people supporting Dr. Jenkins's work are W. Edwards Deming and John Hattie.

Having spoken to educators all across the United States, Latin America, Europe, Australia, and Asia, Lyle Lee Jenkins is passionate about equipping the next generation with a true love of learning.

Dr. Lyle Lee Jenkins holds a Bachelor of Arts degree from Point Loma Nazarene University, a Masters of Education from San Jose State University and a Ph.D. from the Claremont Graduate University.

Lyle Lee Jenkins's website, www.LtoJ.net, is a great place to discover useful tools to guide your educational journey.

ABOUT THE AUTHORS

Do you have a great photo or video of your student using one of our products?

We would love the opportunity to share it on our website and social media channels!

Email us at info@ltoj.net

If you have a story to share, we would also like to hear from you. We feature student stories during presentations and on our social media accounts.

Our team loves sharing the joy of a child understanding new concepts. It allows our audience to experience firsthand the mission our team works towards every day; for students to maintain the same love of learning they brought to Kindergarten throughout all their years of schooling and into adulthood.

Thank you for being a loyal customer. We appreciate you!

The LtoJ Team

Follow us on Instagram, Facebook, TikTok and YouTube
@LtoJLLC

www.ingramcontent.com/pod-product-compliance
Lightning Source LLC
Chambersburg PA
CBHW081006120626
46546CB00010B/3031